The Little Know-How Book

THE LITTLE Know-How BOOK

Everything You Need to Know to Get By in Life from Changing a Tire to Figuring a Tip to Tying Your Shoes

BOB SCHER

Crown Trade Paperbacks
New York

Copyright © 1993 by Robert Scher
Illustrations copyright © 1993 by Richard Sala

Published by Crown Trade Paperbacks, 201 East 50th Street, New York,
New York 10022. Member of the Crown Publishing Group.

Originally published in hardcover by Harmony Books,
a division of Crown Publishers, Inc., in 1993.
First paperback edition published in 1995.

Random House, Inc. New York, Toronto, London, Sydney, Auckland

CROWN TRADE PAPERBACKS and colophon are trademarks of Crown
Publishers, Inc.

Manufactured in the United States of America

Library of Congress Cataloging-in-Publication Data
Scher, Bob.
The little know-how book: everything you need to know to get by in life from
changing a tire to figuring a tip to tying your shoes/Bob Scher.—1st ed.
p. cm.
Originally published: New York: Harmony Books, 1993.
1. Life skills—United States. I. Title.
[HQ2039.I6S34 1994]
306—dc20 94-9666
CIP

ISBN 0-517-88031-8

10 9 8 7 6 5 4 3

To my brother Bill,
who fixes things you don't even
know are broken

Acknowledgments

No one is an island. My thanks to:

Debra Allee, Sally Ashley, Bruce Bixler, Thisbe Blake, Patrick Bromley, Keith Cohn, Connie Cook, Robert Dreyfuss, Maryesther Fournier, Brenda Joynson, Marilyn Koch, Audrey Lee, Dennis Lewis, Dennis Mincieli, Carla Needleman, Richard Owens, Beresford Parlett, Rocky and Karen Price, Sophia Reinders, Charles Siegfried, Barbara Simon, Sophia Stone, Oliver Suzor, Russ Taft, Carol Van Horn, Phil Wood, and all my friends at PeerLogic.

And special praise to my agent, Lizzie Grossman, who wisely drew maps that came true; my editor, John Michel, a bold explorer in disguise; and to loyal friends: Dan and Virginia Gregerson, who consistently made the impossible possible; Carol Pulitzer and Jim Polster, who rescued this effort from oblivion and stood by it; and Nancy, who rescues me from myself, over and over (and over).

Contents

◆ Why I Wrote this Book ◆

There are enormous numbers of books that tell you how to do things, and I've never been able to learn anything from them. The main difficulty with authors of how-to-do-it books is not that they are inarticulate or haven't mastered their subject. On the contrary, they're so thoroughly versed in their area of expertise that they tell me more than I care to know, and yet often they don't reveal the real difficulties.

There are also a great many procedures such as properly changing a fuse, sewing on a button, flying a kite, changing a lamp plug, tying (just) the knots you need, jump-starting your car, opening a defective sardine can (you know the kind I mean, where the tab breaks off after two turns of the key), making friends with (almost) any dog, packing a suitcase, learning enough football terms to follow the announcer, and many other things you never knew you always wanted to know—like tying your shoes so they don't come untied (one quarter of all adults do it wrong), and even how to tuck your shirt in so it won't come out. To most accomplished how-to-do-it persons, many of these activities are so trivial it would embarrass them, and their readers, if they included them in their serious works. Rarely will you find these procedures explained at all—let alone all together in a convenient way.

The Little Know-How Book is more than an out-of-the-ordinary handbook. It is also a survey of some of the fundamental dynamic-world principles that to most how-to-do-it professionals are just bizarre, but to the rest of us are as real as a cold, rainy day. For example:

· *The Principle of Disappearance:* Personal objects shift around by themselves.

· *The Law of Certain Things:* All manufactured items possess an unreasonable power of self-preservation that discourages you and me from simply adjusting them or (God forbid) looking *inside*.

· *The Fear of Being a Public Laughingstock.*

· *The Fear of Death.*

Generally these principles apply to a wide range of activities, but instead of taking each of them up separately, I have incorporated them, or their variations, in suitable places throughout the book.

How to Use this Book: Sticky Points and How-to-Do-It Laws

Many of the instructions are abbreviated and do not include every obligatory step. This is necessary for those of us who have been put off by a task because we feel that we can't follow its maze of instructions completely. Or perhaps we are simply curious about a procedure and just want to have a clear overview.

By putting the major attention on the critical and sticky points—in fact, knowing where they are and where they aren't is half the difficulty—the reader is free to apply the same simple common sense to the easier parts that he or she possesses in other areas of life and in this way even develops some self-confidence.

This is a shocking departure, I know, from the current fashion, which is to baby the reader through every subtle turn. There are always those who like to follow complicated instructions, but the rest of us often end up confused or bored, or we refuse to believe that it's all that complicated and just give up.

◄ *Critical and Sticky Points* ► are marked with a ◄, and various *How-to-Do-It Laws* are scattered throughout. How-to-Do-It Laws can help you develop the poise to cope with situations without having to refer to a book. It's actually possible to follow the instructions and yet be utterly paralyzed if you don't have them in front of you when you have to do something. *The Little Know-How Book* wants you to be able, when at all possible, to walk through life without a reference.

The Great Law of Undoing is an example of a How-to-Do-It Law. This principle can guide you in many a common situation, where what is required is merely to open something up,* do something to it, then close it up (the reverse of opening up).

| **The Great Law of Undoing means:** |
| The Original Condition + Undoing + Doing = The Original Condition |
| (DEFECTIVE)   (FIXED) |

One more example is *The Law of the Richness of Reality*, which in How-to-Do-It World means there is always more than one effective way to do anything. Perhaps you already do something a different way than I suggested. It may even be a better way.

I don't want to know about it. The point is that here you have a simple procedure that works—usually one that has been tried and tested millions, even billions, of times.

You imagine, of course, that the author must have tried to

---

* This is called "to take apart" in regular how-to-do-it books.

determine which way is "best." Only up to a point. Why? Because of the Popover Fallacy:

Cookbook authors will not only swear by their own particular method of making popovers (for example), but they will often claim that certain other methods, which correspond to the favorite method of some other expert, are unacceptable and no self-respecting cook could entertain the possibility of doing it that other way. For instance:

"Forget what you've read elsewhere. The secret in making good popovers is to start them in a cold oven." *

This is complete nonsense. Though this method is perfectly acceptable for making popovers, there are at least ten other ways just as good. (As a matter of fact, my own way is better.)

Finally, there is The Law of Enough. This law tells me that this chapter is over.

---

* *The Fannie Farmer Cookbook, Twelfth Edition*, revised by Marion Cunningham with Jeri Laber (New York: Alfred A. Knopf, 1979), pg. 492.

◆ How to Get Rid of Ants ◆

So you're finally on one of the Ant Trails. They're here and they keep on coming. Don't worry, you can handle it.

How to Do It

1. Clean up. Sugar, honey, meat, food in general—you're crazy if you leave these out in the open. You are *asking* to become a bona fide member of the trail. If you've already got ants, you have to be scrupulous about this. It solves most problems.

> **The Law of Ants:** Ants were put here so that the Fear of Ants (Pretty groundless, unless they're African Army Ants who eat cows and things) would help us become cleaner persons at home.

2. Use ant-sticks. Sprays, ant powder, etc., inside your home are obnoxious. Ant-sticks address the problem at its source, which is the outside, where ants "work the trails" (honestly, they have routes, schedules, assignments, scouts who report, etc., etc.; we're talking military here). Different brands of ant-sticks have different names, but the idea is always the same: They are stakes that go into the ground around the house. You leave them in for a month or so, and you probably won't have to repeat the treatment.

Ant-sticks discourage ants from including your house on their route assignments. Your address gets anted out, your house is considered "a negative-energy non-target location," and you have successfully directed them somewhere else. (Where to, you don't want to know.)

3. Supplement with bay leaves. Put a few around the places where ants come in. After the ant-stick treatment, bay leaves are very effective in banishing the last few wandering ants lost on the old trail.

4. Exception. If you live on a boat or some other un-ant-stickable place, the next level down would be ant traps and bay leaves in your living quarters.

Optional

In exceedingly stubborn situations, one method that is sometimes effective is called Shouting at Ants. For example, "Get out!"

One of the reasons this unorthodox method may work is that the self-embarrassment you feel upon TALKING OUT LOUD TO ANTS is one of the vibrations that ants can't bear, since their lives are based on modestly conforming to a rigidly established norm. Living in a house with an ambivalent exhibitionist is contrary to their sense of order. And so they just leave. (That's the idea, anyway.)

How to Move

◆ ◆

"Three removes is as bad as a fire."
Ben Franklin

How to Self-Pack

The First Law of Packing: No matter how many boxes you think you need, you will need twice as many.

1. Throw things away *before* you move. One of the benefits of moving is throwing—or giving—away things you don't need, really don't want, and will never use again. Oddly enough, once you're in a new home it is very hard to throw anything out. *So do this while packing up.*

2. If there are movers, always make a written inventory of your goods. Transport really important papers yourself.

3. Don't pack books, records, or papers in large boxes. (Ow! My back!)

4. Don't mix kitchen items in with underwear. I.e., *organize.* The more organized you are in packing—without getting fanatical—the better it will be later (note that I didn't say it would necessarily be "good" later).

5. Pack kitchen items individually—except for clusters of silverware—in clear plastic freezer bags of various sizes. These can be recycled (and they work better than brown Kraft paper). They will come out clean on the other end. If you use regular newsprint, you will have to wash each one of them when you unpack. (Movers use unprinted newsprint.)

The Second Law of Packing: Label boxes completely or suffer later.

---

6. Clean thoroughly. Be courteous (also get your cleaning deposit back). If you don't understand the technology of cleaning, then get someone to help you clean for the incoming tenant. Pay special attention to the appliances.

7. Arrange for basic services before you move. Telephone, utilities (gas, electricity, water), garbage pickup. Before you move, or right afterward, identify your daily transportation routes, find a nearby cleaner, and locate your new post office and mail drop. This is utterly simple and incredibly helpful and you would be amazed at how many people don't do it.

——— *Unpacking—Another World* ———

The sprawl of items, and no room. But ever since the invention of moving, the world has eventually shifted around to accommodate new tenants.

1. If you are overwhelmed, first unpack your books and put them away. For some reason, unpacking books clarifies the space and initiates world-shifting.* Nobody knows why this works.

——— *The False Opposites* ———

That little two-letter prefix "un" that "unpacking" starts with might fool you into thinking that unpacking is merely the reverse of packing.

The Law of Unpacking: If packing and unpacking were opposites, then all the laws of physics would have to be totally redone.

In fact, these two activities are *False Opposites*. Unpacking (an enormous process that takes most people at least a month) is at least 7^3 times more difficult than packing, which consists simply of the ability to shmush things into boxes and bags in some kind of order.

* It also makes us feel better.

9

Unpacking involves some unpleasant activities:

2. You must *constantly face* looking at useless objects. These were the items you were unable to throw away.

3. You must *make decisions*. This is a subset of personal thinking—like "Where do I put the trapezoidal table?" and so on.

4. You will almost certainly have to *buy lamps*. (One of the most exasperating laws is *The Law of Lamps*, which is that most lamps displayed in lamp stores are totally inappropriate in your home.)

5. Think before you place. Usually, only a couple of reasonable locations work for any sizable object. Think it all through, using a *tape measure* (math!) to determine what normal or ingenious arrangements are possible. Of course, any object can be moved later and you should count on some changing about because on-site looking is *truth in furniture*.

──────── *Not Really Optional* ────────

Finally, do not move until you *believe* what is said about lifting in "Three Vital Ways to Preserve Your Back," pg. 15. This is not a joke.

◆ A Primer on How to Look at Art ◆

"With an apple I will astonish Paris."
Paul Cezanne

We begin with the number-one truth: No matter what you or I believe, *everything*—including all possible spaces and all possible times, whether obviously connected or not—*is a part of one fantastically great whole.* Every visual and musical composition—every well-made object—reflects this and, in some sense, invokes its own "micro-world." (I don't have space at this time for opposing arguments.)

11

Art—A World of Space

Lets look at just one fundamental aspect of the above truth. Though this fact is of the greatest importance visually, artistically, and even "cosmologically," it is often noted only as an intriguing attribute of some particular painting or photograph or style (e.g., when talking about the *Mona Lisa* or a Chinese painting). But it permeates every visual creation at the primary level. It is the artistic requirement to open up to, or literally to see, the *invisible*.

Hey, that's a blatant contradiction!

Visible + Invisible = The Whole Picture

Usually we fixate on, or are distracted by, some object or objects in a picture—especially ones that we deem to be, or are "told," is the "subject matter." It's what's over there when you say, "Look at that!" It's called *positive* space.

But in a picture, even though we don't usually think about it, we also experience *empty* space, like the spaces around the various "things that are there." (Some wise person has renamed this *negative* space.) Now as long as we experience this negative space as less important than "the things that are there"—the positive space, which takes most of our attention—we deprive ourselves of a more fundamental encounter with the picture, because in art these two spaces are both significant, inseparable, and in a sense equal. A painting asks us to "Look" not just to "Look at that."

In some situations, like in painting, Everything Counts. Just as you can't throw out a chunk of "world" (since everything is "world," where would you toss it?), you have to *include* it.

A Tutorial

The *Mona Lisa* is "reproduced" (pg. 11)—well, approximately. (Better yet, look up your own reproduction of Leonardo's painting in a book.) In this case we are presented not only with negative space, but also with a *background*. This "background," just like empty or negative space, is often considered just the "background," and somehow counts for less than the "real" subject matter.

Instead of rattling on about the mystery woman, her enigmatic smile, her intriguing hands, etc., we shall instead focus on the negative space and the background. And what a background!

1. Consider the sky that surrounds the figure as a *shape*. In this case, the sky is not only above, but appears between many of the remarkable rock shapes. Try now to look at the whole picture as a design of *shapes*, including the negative spaces.

2. Observe how the "background" both blends with and recedes from the foreground. Note how the cliffs, the spires, the hint of oceanic distance, the subtle cloud forms, and so on, either directly harmonize with the foreground (e.g., the distant curving paths suggest the curves of the garment—even the shape of the face) or dynamically set it off.

3. Alternate looking at the background separately, then together with the foreground. Of course, in the case of the *Mona Lisa* the whole concept of the "background" is a *tour de force*. (The "fantastic," mythical landscape with a profound, almost mythical person in the foreground is, among other things, a powerful reminder of the significance of "backgrounds.")

Eventually we can almost "feel" the quality of *light and*

13

space in the painting. I don't mean some obvious 3-D effect, but rather—this is harder to explain than to actually observe—a sense of the whole medium in which every painting lives, around and between everything, including the background.

Most art books that go into raptures over the *Mona Lisa* spend very little, if any, of their allotted space on a discussion of the background (which only strengthens our point). Yet without the background, this painting would be a splendid portrait and not the transcendent masterpiece that it is.

We can learn even more from paintings and photographs that don't quite work. Many student paintings—even when the figures, the proportions, and so on, are all well composed—often have backgrounds that are not in a dynamic relationship with the "subject matter." But as the painter or photographer matures, the backgrounds begin to operate as a vital force in the picture, whether boldly or subtly harmonized with the other elements. In master paintings and photographs, the whole space vibrates with life.

Sure, there are critical factors like line, color, direction, texture, associations, and so on (an enormous list); but if you begin to practice seeing in this fundamental way, the more you look, the more the other critical elements will reveal themselves to you, separately and together. And you will enter more and more easily into the real presence of the painting.

Three Vital Ways to
Preserve Your Back

◆ ◆

Carrying Wallets

1. Guys, take your wallets out of your back pockets. Chiropractors (and orthopedists) are taking considerable amounts of money out of your wallet just because you're keeping it in your back pocket. Stuffing your wallet in there can destabilize your back. This is easy to test. Sit down with your wallet in its usual place. Now remove the wallet.

Feel the difference? You should. But even if you don't, there *is* a difference, a *tremendous* difference. Imagine the unbalanced pressure on your skeleton—moment after moment, hour after hour, day in, day out. Ask a structural engineer or somebody. Believe me, it's a *fact*, and most chiropractors and orthopedists would be the first to tell you.

Lifting Heavy Things

2. If you aren't accustomed to it, do not suddenly begin lifting or hauling huge things. *Work up to it.* Back problems are epidemic, and not heeding this advice is one of the main reasons why the *majority* of doctor's visits in the United States are musculoskeletal related. If you suffer from a recurring back problem, don't be embarrassed to ask for help when lifting something heavy, or even to pay someone to help you.* Lifting can be healthy—humans

---

* But heeding this advice is guaranteed cheaper than professional treatment.

weren't invented just to sit around all the time—but you have to use common muscular sense.

Now most people know that when lifting something heavy, they should bend their knees. But that's not all.

3. When lifting, you should bend your knees, and keep your back straight.* That is, you should *squat*. Squatting, unfortunately, is pooh-poohed by many Westerners—maybe it's the sound of the word—but it's an invigorating posture. Just straighten your knees to come up.

You can sense immediately that there is less strain and more power available, but most of us never discover this.

Exercise

I'm not qualified to tell *you*, specifically, what your exercise program should be. Still, I do know that we need to maintain musculature not only in the lower back but also in the abdomen, for weakness there encourages back problems. Check out one of the existing 5 million exercise or stretching books.

Just as significant, there are sound ways to reach, stand, stoop, and sit that have now become more widely know. For example, when reaching up, don't lock your knees—keep them slightly bent. Locking your knees has no effect on how high you can reach. (Try it.) And considering the daily amount of sitting that goes on, knowing more about this should be a priority—more vital perhaps than knowing what a politician says he or she will do for you next year.

For example, sitting for an extended period without breaks —especially in a bad chair—is known to put a strain on the lower back. More and more car seats are appearing with lumbar support. But we're still in the primitive stage. Bad

* There is a normal curve in the lower back (the "lordosis") that is properly preserved when your back is "straight."

16

car seats can produce as bad a back as an ill-toted wallet. If your car seat, or your *office* seat, encourages inordinate slouching, consider your long-range health and then consider checking out a small back pillow.

Hey, but a real man doesn't use a back pillow! (You better find out how many "real men" end up with back problems and stoopage.) More and more people are wising up.

How to Barbecue on the Open Grill

A human being is an animal that barbecues.

Barbecuing is one of those activities that produces marvelous results way beyond our efforts. Of course, barbecuing is just plain cooking—the very same laws apply. And the great thing about barbecuing is that whether you are a cook or not, you can barbecue right away and produce delicious results. In fact, it's twice as easy as you think, since the margins of error are great and kind. But it's also twice as real—there is heat, smoke, and (nonthreatening) flames! action!!

How to Do It

I'm assuming that you have some sort of home grill and that you're going to use charcoal briquettes (or mesquite charcoal —or even hardwood), sold almost everywhere.

1. Have ready: pot holders, a squirt bottle of water, and tongs. (Don't use a fork to turn meat or you will poke holes and lose juice.)

The Fire

2. Heat up the coals before lighting them up. When ready to put on the food, spread the coals out—a little wider than the cooking area. A few of the many ways to heat up the grill:

Small, compressed wood pieces. These are found where briquettes are sold—they ignite easily and will start the briquettes going without fuss. Ready to grill in about 30 minutes.

Electric starter. This is very easy, very clean, environmentally correct, and inexpensive (you can reuse). Place the starter on some new or leftover coals from last time, pile coals up over the starter, and remove the device 10 minutes

18

later. After 20 minutes, you can begin grilling.

Liquid charcoal starter. This weird substance may pollute the taste of your meal. Be sure to use one that is specified for charcoal cooking, and use it only as a last resort.

3. Manage the heat. This is the ongoing primary challenge in all of cooking. When grilling you use judgment, but you have a good amount of (raw and ex-raw) data right there in front of you.

You can raise or lower the heat during the cooking using any of the following methods.

4. Wait until the briquettes are entirely covered with gray ash. The ash insulates and produces a medium-low and steady heat. If you require a higher temperature, say for grilling a steak, you can knock off some of the ash. To lower the heat, spread out the coals. You can increase/decrease the heat by raising/lowering the grate, or performing whatever other clever procedures your equipment allows. You can also add briquettes every 30 or 45 minutes to keep the heat relatively constant.

By the way, cooking writers estimate cooking temperature based on how far they can *count* while keeping a hand over the grill. You know what? After barbecuing a few times, your hand will know how hot the grill is directly, without any counting. (Many of my readers are allergic to math, not to mention excessive heat.)

Fat

5. For lean meat, like spareribs (or chicken), rub the grill with fat.

6. If the meat is fatty (e.g., sirloin steak), to avoid curling, slash the edge-fat every couple inches. But do not cut into the meat. Cut off excess fat; otherwise, it will drip into the coals and create a very smoky fire in your pit, though some will drip down anyway. (Where's the squirt bottle?)

The Grilling

DONENESS

Lean meat definitely needs marinating, basting, and longer, slower cooking. Spareribs should be well-cooked for an hour, or even longer.

Other meats, such as a sirloin steak or hamburger, can be grilled plain over hot coals or smeared with your favorite sauce. Steak is ready to turn when beads of juice appear on top. When it comes to being done, ◄ never be embarrassed to cut into meat to see if it's finished the way you want it. ►

SEARING

Red meat and poultry can benefit from searing. Why not experiment? At the beginning, lower the meat to about 2 or 3 inches from the hot coals for 2 or 3 minutes.

Marinating/Basting

A typical **marinade** is similar to a salad dressing—vinegar or wine; oil; and herbs and spices—but usually with a higher proportion of vinegar or (red) wine. You can also use fruit juice, tomatoes, sweet, sour—and your imagination. ◄ In a glass or enamel container, bring the meat to room temperature ► and place in the marinade for at least 2 to 4 hours, turning several times. You can also use marinades for **basting,** to moisten and impart flavor when grilling.

Fish

Salmon, trout, and other fatty fish are superb when grilled and require nothing but a little oil. However, you can certainly baste them with fish compatibles such as the famous lemon, butter, and herbs, without masking the flavor. Turn once. Fish is done when it flakes in its thickest part.

Chicken on the Open Grill

The Law of Barbecued Chicken Pieces: "They're not done yet."

This interminable cooking time for chicken means that you don't want too hot a fire or you may burn the outside and leave the inside undercooked. Horrible charred things are really not healthy to eat. But I did *not* say to *undercook* the chicken! (Awful.) There should be no pink near the bone. ◄ Do not be afraid to cut next to a bone and look. ► (One easy trick is to microwave the chicken for just a few minutes since this cooks the juicy areas near the bone first. However, some cooks would never mix microwaving with barbecuing.)

Chicken can take much basting. And chicken pieces are not nice and flat but weirdly shaped so they usually need cooking on the edges. At some point, you can lean them up against themselves. Allow 15 to 20 minutes for breasts (to keep them from drying out, keep basting), and up to 45 minutes for whole legs with thighs (these are excellent).

Since a chicken's shape demands more than a single turning, the true, bracing challenge of those important words "Turn the chicken occasionally" is a secret known only to those who have barbecued chicken, basting with an over-oily sauce in a constantly shifting wind. Step lively, mate.

How to Make Your Bed

There are two good ways to make a bed, depending on your life history up to this moment.

The Body Bed

Take the top blanket, or a quilt, and drape it over the entire bed and don't do anything else. The effect is "There is a body in the bed."

This method is fine if:

Your parents aren't coming over.

You don't have time to make your bed "properly."

You aren't expecting a romantic visitor.

None of your anticipated visitors is in law enforcement.

You don't remember in the depths of your being that getting under the covers of a properly made bed is very special and helps you sleep better.

The Proper Bed

Now, I realize that everyone has a method, or non-method, for making a bed, and I am not going to attempt to alter such firmly entrenched habits. But everyone knows how much time is spent in bed, so this qualifies as an important issue.

Some like a tight bed; some like it loose. Some burrow into their covers; others flail and unmake the bed almost immediately. A few fine points:

1. Make sure the sheet is high enough up at the top. Otherwise the sleeper may have to pull the whole sheet out, and up, to cover his or her shoulders.

2. Make sure that the blanket doesn't go up as high as the sheet. Otherwise, when the sleeper gets in, the blanket will be next to skin. A blanket next to skin drives some people temporarily insane.

Of course, if you have a comforter or duvet, this section is irrelevant since your method will be similar to The Body Bed, only we hope you will use a little more care.

Why did *everybody* make such a big deal out of the obligatory, arch-dreaded HOSPITAL CORNERS? It's actually more difficult *not* to make them. Of course, if you don't want a tight bed, you may not even want to tuck in the sheets and blankets at the foot.

I must confess that my usually wise and patient editor observed that I had not described how to actually produce hospital corners and he was understandably shocked.* But it happens to be one of those very simple procedures that needs too many words to describe. (He has just informed me that I cannot get out of this with that excuse.) Okay.

After tucking in the sheet at the foot of the bed, make a hospital corner on each side: **(1)** With one hand, lift up the sheet four or five inches from the corner. **(2)** With the other hand, tuck in the part of the sheet between the first hand and the corner. **(3)** Finally, tuck in the part of the sheet held by the first hand, which will *fold over* the part you previously tucked in.

* "You're not going to include hospital corners?"

How to Ride a Ten-Speed Bicycle

Some of us grew up on bicycles, from one-speed and up. They were as close to being a part of our bodies as blue jeans. Yet many owners of ten-speed bicycles today are unschooled and confused about some of the basics.

Safety

Sooner or later you are going to ride on a street with other vehicles. There is a nonburdensome *technology* of safety, and it is important for you (and your children) that you learn about it. Bicycle shops have material and so does your library. You will be surprised to discover that many of the safety notions you believe in *are proven mistakes*.

Brakes

Different riders may have different opinions about how to use the brakes. But most would agree with the following:

1. Know which lever works which brake. (Some riders actually don't know.)

2. Apply equal and *gradual* pressure on both brakes, bringing in the rear brake *slightly before* the front brake. (You will probably do this instinctively.) The front brake provides two to three times more traction than the rear brake (watch how a dog stops in his or her tracks). But if you use just the front brake—or use it before the rear brake—you could find yourself on the other side of the handlebars.

Pedaling

3. Pedal in circles. Imagine yourself providing power with your legs the whole way around. Be aware of how your calves and hamstrings are helping. You will quickly discover how much better it is pedaling this way. (Toe clips can help, which reminds me that if you are a beginner, be sure your toe and not your instep works the pedal.)

4. Don't pump the pedals. This means don't push *down* with one foot, then *down* with the other foot (perhaps even "standing up"). It's the exact opposite of how to ride most efficiently, pleasantly, and with the least fatigue. Why is this? Because if you aren't helping your idle or upward-moving leg *to lift up*, then it will act as a weight on the pedal causing your downward-moving leg to work much harder. Learning this may take some practice, but it's worth it.

> **The Law of Animal Movement:** Imagine yourself moving the way you would like to move. (Athletes and dancers all do this whether they know it or not.)

5. Try to maintain a consistent tempo of pedaling. Use the gear that lets you do this. Some riders assume that the higher the gear, the more speed, efficiency, and exercise they are gaining. This is wrong. The rate of pedaling is what counts.

Depending on your condition, begin with a pace of normal walking (in engineering jargon this is about 60 revolutions per minute), but you eventually want to go somewhat faster —then everything gets easier. Your feet will feel as if they're spinning around. You get less tired and are much more efficient than when you were pushing against a hard, high gear with your feet moving through molasses—which is also punishing on various body parts, like your knees, for example.

Gears

6. Frequent shifting is normal.

7. Practice on a level road, starting with the large chain and the middle sprocket. Try different gear combinations, ◄ shifting up and down one gradation at a time. ► (Of course, on a ten-speed you shift gears *only* while pedaling.*) You paid for the gears so use them. But you really have only eight gears, because . . .

8. There are two gear combinations you should generally avoid: Large outside to large inside, and small inside to small outside. This means when the chain goes from the outside, large front chainwheel to the inside (large) rear sprocket, or from the small to the small. In these cases, you are putting strain on the chain because it is crossing the bicycle at the most extreme angles. These are mid-range gears that are essentially duplicated by other combinations. Also you probably won't use your highest gear except when being pushed by a strong wind at your back, or when going downhill, and you'll most likely reserve your lowest gear for climbing steep hills. Note: If these gears are shifting noisily, have them checked out.

9. Downshift *before* you come to a hill or traffic light. Shifting ahead is efficient. Don't wait until your feet feel like blocks of concrete.

Believe it or not, you'll soon have your own repertoire of gear use, secretly whispered to you by your bicycle itself.

---

* On a three-speed, when *not* pedaling.

Emergency Stopping

1. Apply both brakes simultaneously, but with two or three times as much force on the front brake. The moment your *rear* wheel begins skidding—this is a sign that it's about to lift up—let up on the front brake and transfer effort to the rear. Practice.*

2. If you start to skid, *release* the brakes until your wheel starts rolling, then reapply. *Do not grip the brakes more firmly.*

Emergency Turning

If you have to turn suddenly, say to avoid an oncoming car, you must do something that at first seems counter-intuitive. But after practicing, it becomes natural.

1. Begin with a slight turn in the *wrong* direction.

2. Then quickly turn back in the desired direction.†

Once you learn all these things, they seem as natural as walking. Of course, walking was never a big deal. You were given a body with all the latest technology, and after crawling around for a while, one day you just decided to stand up and walk. (Somehow, this doesn't seem accurate.)

---

* The school parking lot is the traditional place.
† What's happening here? When you make that first turn, the accelerating forces involved in Newton's Second Law of Motion (a change in speed *or* direction implies acceleration) cause you to lean in the *opposite* direction—that of the desired turn. Leaning is a major element in negotiating a successful turn.

Getting to the Next Plateau of Birds

"The world should listen then, as I am listening now."
Percy Bysshe Shelley, from "To a Skylark"

Small Talk

Probably no other conversation with strangers is more productive than, say, "Did you know that a swift often spends twenty-four hours flying around in the sky without stopping and eats insects on the wing? That it can travel almost a thousand miles a day and not complain?"

There is no end with birds. Yet most of us can discriminate only *eight* backyard birds. Some folks go all the way up to *twelve*, depending on which children's books they remember. (This is *The Law of Birds*.)

But just reflect on the utter wonder of our flying companions—and that they are the most accessible, wild, warm-blooded creatures that untrained people like you and me can observe close up in their natural habitats. And these untethered spirits ecologically eliminate more insect pests than any chemical we have ever concocted. If the birds disappeared, so probably would we, because in a few years the insects, multiplying beyond belief, would devour every growing plant. Even one bird in your area graces you with more peace of mind than you may ever realize.

The Eight Backyard Birds You Know

1. Robin—a thrush. The robin is a "standard bird" because the sizes of other small and medium-sized birds are measured by it: two-thirds of a robin, one and a half robins, and so forth.

2. Cardinal—a finch. Lucky you if they live in your region. (They don't migrate.) They're *more* spectacular than their pictures, and their song is clear, flute-like, and memorable. I have heard them answer one another over great distances. Cardinals are the state bird of a record seven states. (And they're on STAMPS!)

3. Crow—a member of the crow (Corvidus) family. Crows can eat practically anything. And apart from its genius relative, the slightly larger raven, the crow is our most intelligent bird, hands down.* In the legendary Farmer Wars, the poor farmers were never a match for the crows. They tried to decimate them with rifles, poison—and bombs! —but the crows kept cropping up.

No other bird is the subject of so many contradictory descriptions. Crows usher untold numbers of insects into the afterworld, so they probably deserve to eat some of the corn that they themselves preserve. (Understandably, farmers don't see it that way.) Like most birds, crows are caring and meticulous with their young. They are also very friendly with one another, even when feeding.

RAVEN NOTE: Some of the Northwest Indians, like the Kwakiutl, considered the Raven the most sacred and wise of

---

* Scientists claim that birds are even smarter than dogs. However, if you are lost in the woods, would you rather have them send out a dog—or a *bird?*

all creatures. But all *we* got was "The Raven."*

4. Bluejay—a member of the crow family. Domineering, raucous—and strikingly blue. To some, the jay is a pest, yet they warn neighboring birds of danger, eat their share of insects, and, like squirrels, bury nuts and acorns, thus creating multitudes of trees.

5. Sparrow—a member of the sparrow/finch family, the largest family of birds. You can recognize a sparrow not only by its size, shape, streaks of brown, and its strong, *stubby beak*, but also by the way it *hop-hops*, just like, well, a sparrow. Regular sparrows eat megatons of weed seeds, which is very good for farmers (but not for weeds). Some, like the song sparrow, sing delightfully.

6. Hummingbird—a member of the swift family. The hummingbird is certainly a candidate for one of the Top Ten Living Earth Beings: (1) They eat *nectar;* (2) they can hover motionless except for their wings, which beat faster than most airplane propellers rotate; (3) they build expert nests (many birds are actually sloppy); and (4) some are even *iridescent.* Hummingbirds obviously live in such a rapidly vibrating world that you can imagine what one of them might say when it notices

ONE OF US COMING ALONG

"Hey, here comes one of those dumb, zombie monsters moving at 4.2 millimeters a [hummingbird] minute."

* Poe wrote a few very fine poems, many great short stories, and excellent criticism. But only a deluded English teacher would mistake his droll doggerel "The Raven" as anything but joke verse. It's an intentionally bloated, fake-o, baloney poem, a good humorous lyric (in spite of its "somber" subject): "What this grim, ungainly, ghastly, gaunt, and ominous bird of yore/Meant in croaking 'Nevermore.' " Give us a break. W. S. Gilbert would have written it if he had to spend the night in the Winchester Mystery House. And then we would have had Sullivan's music! ("Was this big and bellicose, broad and bumpy, bawdy gal Lenore/Baking biscuits on the floor?" from "Lenore and the Raven.")

31

7. Woodpecker. A remarkable concept in bird technology. (They have *zygodactyl feet*—for your investigation.)

8. Swallow—not a swift. Everyone knows swallows, gracefully gliding or lining up on telephone wires. But only the barn swallow has the forked "swallow tail" pictured in children's books.

_ *Blurred Knowledge of Four—You* _ *May Know, or You May Not*

9. Wren. It's a small, plump bird with a *cocked tail* and a delightful song. The wren is one of the birds for whom we build a specific house (a wren house). We build them—or mostly, we buy them—and they come!

10. Starling. It has a short tail and darkly iridescent body. It flocks in large numbers and seriously interferes with aircraft.

11. Chickadee. It joyfully sings its "name" in every kind of weather, year round. It has a black or brownish cap and bib.

12. Red-winged blackbird. It has red epaulets on its shoulders. This is more than just for show. These birds will defend their nests to the death against snakes and larger predators.

Others

Of course we know *about* goldfinches, mockingbirds, nuthatches, meadowlarks, skylarks (not found in the United States), warblers, vireos, whippoorwills, phoebes, purple finches, bobolinks, bobwhites, buntings, juncos, flycatchers, grackles, purple martins, kingbirds, wood thrushes, etc.

Please get a bird book! Binoculars are optional but help-ful. Be soft and quiet around birds.

— *Who Is the Greatest (U.S.) Singer?* —

Many say it is the hermit thrush. From invisible depths in the midst of the woods, an exquisite song sails upward while the notes float downward. (The nightingales of Europe—and fairy tales—are at least equally marvelous.)

A Little Extra

The next time you feel a little too tired or too hassled to take the garbage out or type that letter or tell your child a story, you might remember the chimney swift up there, flapping and flying as we speak.

◆ How to Treat Minor Burns ◆

Clearly this is not a medical manual, but everyone should know how to treat minor burns (we're talking *minor* here). These are usually acquired in the kitchen, or when trying to change a light bulb with your bare hands (while it's on).

HISTORY

For hundreds, thousands of years, normal humans, upon receiving one of their life's allotted burns, have desired to plunge the affected appendage into cold water, and the colder the better. Ice water is very good.

Now, Western medical doctors are right plenty of times,

but they apparently didn't know about this until 1962 when it was finally deemed an "official way" to treat minor burns.

WHAT TO DO
Plunge the affected part into cold water/ice water, and leave it in for ten or fifteen minutes. This is the best way to avoid a blister.

HOW IT WORKS
One of the reasons that this is so effective—aside from the obvious effect of the cold that helps stop the burning—is the lack of air reaching the burn. It is surprising how many doctors don't know about this. However chemists, when receiving one of their designated burns, instinctively, immediately, completely cover the burn (for starters, with their other hand) to keep the air from encouraging an oxidation proc . . . oh, you don't want to know about this.

Yet nothing seems to beat ice water.

◆ How to Sew a Button on a Shirt ◆

Please take just a moment of your life to consider sewing. No craft is more necessary or more profound. It was not a frivolous impulse that caused the Greeks to associate the Fates with sewing.* While the rest of us go off and noisily scrub, hammer, compute, and make deposits, the sewers quietly stitch things together.

* Well, at least, with the spinning of thread. A Fate named Clotha was in charge of this. (See *The Encyclopedia Britannica*)

34

How to Do It

1. Use about a foot and a half of strong thread.

2. Thread the needle (help!), pull both ends together, and tie a knot. Moisten the thread knife-point sharp for easier insertion into the ancient EYE OF THE NEEDLE. There is usually a little groove right next to the eye, parallel to the needle, that you can feel with your finger (many people don't know about this). You can use this to aim the thread. Of course, you can also buy a threader for next to nothing, which makes it easier, i.e., you can give up. No blame.

3. Place the button carefully. A button off-line is unpleasant.

4. Bring the needle from the underside up through a hole, then down through a different hole.* Do three of these loops through these two holes and finish underneath. Repeat for the two remaining holes.

5. Make a simple knot. To do this, stitch the needle through the thread gathered underneath, leaving some slack for a loop, then put the needle back through this loop. Repeat to make a double knot.

6. Snip off the unneeded thread. Or *bite* off the thread with your *teeth*. No, wait! Some youngsters were aggressively admonished by dentists never to bite thread with teeth, notwithstanding that millions of people at this very instant *are biting thread with teeth*. However, it really may be true that these dentists were right. I suggest playing it safe, unless you're already an inveterate thread-biter.†

---

* There are Schools of Sewing Thought here, but any order of hole selection works. How about matching stitches on the buttons already there?

† Of course, some enterprising floss company could manufacture dental floss in the form of button-sewing thread, and now you have a billion-dollar idea for free.

What Not to Forget When You Go Camping

♦ ♦

Even if you read this very carefully, you are still almost certain to forget something. And if this is your first camping trip, it might be an important item, like the tent.

Don't lose heart. This happens because there is a powerful law, *The Law of Saucers*, unknown to you until now.

The Law of Saucers

You enter a coffeehouse and order a cappuccino. Directly involved is a cup, a saucer, a spoon, chocolate or cinnamon (or both if you're a pig), a napkin, and, of course, the drink! The Law of Saucers means that the universe rarely allows objects just to be plunked down on one another, or shmushed together without mercy. There are *intermediate agents*, such as the ligaments between muscle and bone, spoons to stir things together, and saucers underneath coffee cups, that do the very important jobs of transitioning and altogether help make the world subtle and harmonious and, actually, livable.

Now the cup, the saucer, and the spoon have to be washed. The napkin is crumpled and eventually burned. The chocolate and cinnamon shakers are washed or wiped, and refilled continually. In other words, there is always more to do and extra items to get when setting up even very modest conditions.

36

It, therefore, stands to reason that anyone transporting a related assortment of at least five or six objects—especially the first time out—will forget something. So instead of feeling guilty afterward, ask your spouse to read this chapter.

To apply the wisdom embodied here, after collecting your items ask yourself, "What did I forget?" Then . . .

1. Double-check your list.

2. Triple-check those items without which you will trigger search parties with dogs. (See "How to Make Friends with Almost Any Dog," pg. 52.) Your short list might consist of (1) matches, (2) knife, (3) sleeping bag, and in some situations (4) canteen and (5) flashlight (since matches may be precious).

The following is a list of basic items, including some that are often forgotten. Adapt it to your situation.

HOW-TO-DO-IT LIST

flashlights with good batteries (extra batteries for long trips)
knife, Swiss-army knife or equivalent
first-aid kit/medicines
matches, waterproof matches (or spread *nail polish* on your
   kitchen matches)
hatchet, axe
rain gear (especially when you're leaving on a beautiful day)
sunglasses, sunscreen, hats
compass, small mirror
tent, rope, string
sleeping bags, ground cover/air mattress/foam pad
change of underwear/socks/handkerchief

proper boots/shoes
soap, soap dish (or substitute)
laundry soap (if near poison ivy or poison oak)
emergency funds

FOOD RELATED

thermos/canteen
cooking utensils, ladle
bottle opener, can opener
paper towels/toilet paper/trash bags
charcoal, starter
butter (or mock-equivalent) and oil, butter-container (think about summer)
salt and pepper
sugar, syrup, etc.
coffee, tea
possible herbs, spices, sauces (e.g., mustard)
trail mix (this is a kind of granola, which you may find dreadful to eat more than once a year unless you actually consume it on the trail, in which case it is delicious)
other food/special needs (e.g., vitamins)
water/other drinks
more matches in a different place

How to Jump-Start a Car—Even
◆ If You Don't Know What ◆
a Wire Is

". . . the quick and the dead."
The Bible

Your battery has croaked. (You left the lights on all night or
something. Every human being who has owned a car has
done this exact thing.) It's cold as blazes (a weird metaphor),
and you've just pulled this book out of your glove compartment. Your friend has handed you his or her pair of jumper
cables, *both of which are the same color*, with a "clip" at
each of the four ends.* *How do I know which clip goes
where?* (Your friend can't remember either.)

* More and more often, jumper cables come with one red cable and one black. This
brilliant invention is discussed under "Optional."

How to Do It

You need two cars: a living car and, obviously, a dead car. (It's somehow funny that the process won't work without a dead car.)

1. Make sure that both cars have the *same voltage* batteries. Most cars today have 12-volt batteries installed.*

2. Position the living car so that its hood is near that of the dead car. (The cars should *not* touch.)

3. Turn off both ignitions and all electric accessories, such as lights.

4. Open the hoods of both cars and clip one end of either cable onto the positive (+) battery terminal of the living car. Clip the other end of the same cable to the positive (+) terminal of the dead car. Then do the same with the other cable for both the *negative (−)* terminals.

Some knowledgeable people say that to ground everything properly, it is best to clip the *negative (−) cable* in the dead car onto some part of the *engine chassis*. I must also say that neither I nor anyone I know (nor any garage mechanic that I know) has ever clipped this jumper cable to anything other than the NEGATIVE TERMINAL in the dead car. But apparently we are, in fact, wrong about this. It's just that if you panic because you're not sure where the chassis is (it's the big engine thing under the hood), then hook it to the battery. But to be responsible, I have included the engine chassis as the preferred clipping place.

5. Start the engine of the living car and let it run for a while. Then start the engine of the dead car.

---

* The BATTERY is a large (used to be black) rectangular solid presence under your hood (or sometimes under a seat) with two large visible nuts on top called TERMINALS. A 12-volt battery is about the length and width of a standard 8½″ x 11″ piece of paper, or slightly smaller. A 6-volt battery (not as common) is roughly half the size.

When the dead car—suddenly now living car #2—is running, then disconnect the cables in the reverse order you clipped them on. (If the dead car won't start, you can try to rev up the engine of living car #1 by momentarily pressing down on the gas pedal.)

6. Don't turn off the engine of the formerly dead car (now living car #2) until you have driven it for at least half an hour. Unless you plan on continuing to drive it for two or three more hours, take it to any service station and have the battery properly recharged.

The Breakthrough

After the ordeal, take a moment to realize the following: You know at least 500 billion English or other language words (any number more than 100,000 is, for all practical purposes, infinite), countless baseball trivia, sewing nuances, typing motions, and social posturings, and even how to operate a radio in a stupor, *yet, given only two choices, you can never remember which clip goes to which terminal*. Does the positive go to the positive or the negative? With this simple rhyme, those wishy-washy thoughts are now figments of your past.

PLUS TO PLUS WILL START THE BUS.

Complete mastery in less than a page.

Optional

Of course, the whole previous section is almost unnecessary if you possess "intelligent" jumper cables. "Intelligent" means that one cable is red and the other, black. So all you have to remember is that RED is POSITIVE because RED is HOT. Then you know how to hook them all up without poetry.

I should also remind you that keeping (intelligent) cables in your car may not only help you, but may also help someone else in need.

A Formerly Secret Method
◆ for Pleasantly ◆
Ventilating Your Car

I never cease being surprised at the number of drivers who don't know about this.

You have rolled down the driver's-side window to get some fresh air. To prevent unpleasant "car wind" from blasting you in the face as you zing down the highway, while at the same time to encourage fresh air to circulate pleasantly throughout the interior . . .

ALSO ROLL DOWN THE REAR WINDOW ON THE SAME SIDE.

Optional Query

As far as I know, no owner's manual explains this simple and admirable procedure.

Why not?

◆ How to Know the Centuries ◆

*"Oh, no man knows
Through what wild centuries
Roves back the rose."*
Walter de la Mare, from "All That's Past"

Humans in general, and Americans in particular, have an underdeveloped sense of history. For example, out of the last ten centuries, most of us aren't sure which one was known for what. We studied history in school—we even took *tests*. Unfortunately, for many of us, that didn't work. Let's try another approach.

The raw material comes primarily from a famous book, *The Timetables of History*,* which looks at what happened in each year of recorded history—or in the case of earlier eras, in blocks of centuries. Though it is heavily weighted toward the history of Europe, the emphasis is on comparing, in any given year, what was going on in parallel in seven major spheres of human life.

The material here is drawn from the category of "daily life," a selected chronology of momentous occasions in human history. Most of us would agree, for example, that in 750 A.D. "the dukedom of Bavaria extends to Carniola"† is simply not as interesting, or even as important, as the fact that in that year France and Germany got *beds*.

---

* *The Timetables of History*, by Bernard Grun (New York: Simon & Schuster, 1991) (after *Kulturfahrplan*, by Werner Stein).
† Ibid.

A (MOSTLY) EUROPEAN HISTORY UP TO MODERN TIMES

3000–2501 B.C.	Woof! First reports of domesticated dogs in Egypt.
2500–2001 B.C.	The oldest pictorial representation of skiing carved on a rock found in southern Norway.
1500–1001 B.C.	Regulations on the sale of beer in Egypt.
800–701 B.C.	Unisex clothing in Assyria.
600–501 B.C.	Tightly fitting leather clothes in Persia. (The more things change, the more they stay the same.)
43 A.D.	London founded.
50 A.D.	Romans get soap from the Gauls. (And before this?)
600 (ca.)	Zero invented in India and elsewhere, one of humanity's major achievements (inexplicably not in book).
650	Caliphs come out with the first organized news service.
748	China puts first printed newspaper on the stands in Peking.
750	Beds at last! They're popular now in France and Germany.
802	Rose trees first planted in Europe. (The Wars of the Roses came 650 years later.)
850	The Arabian goatherd Kaldi discovers coffee.
963	London Bridge known to exist.
1000	In Europe, "Widespread Fear of the End of the World and the Last Judgment."* The Chinese perfect gunpowder.
1094	Gondolas in Venice.

* *The Timetables of History.*

44

1180	Glass windows in English private homes.
1200	Engagement rings are fashionable.
1220	Giraffes first exhibited in Europe.
1250	Hats are in! So are goose-quill pens.
1290	Spectacles invented.
1305	The yard and the acre are standardized by an English king.
1332, 1347–1351	Bubonic Plague (the Black Death) starts in India and spreads. Between 1347 and 1351 it devastates Europe, killing 75 million people, including one-third of the English population.
1351	The English start playing tennis outdoors.
1450	Mocha, in southwest Arabia, becomes main port for exporting coffee.
1480	Leonardo da Vinci invents the parachute. (Unfortunately, no one has invented the airplane.)
1500	First black-lead pencils in England.
1503	We get the pocket handkerchief! Zanzibar becomes a Portuguese colony.
1514	Europe gets pineapples, all of which is building to a crescendo:
1517	Coffee appears in Europe!!
1560	A come-down: Visiting cards first used by German students.
1568	Bottled beer invented by the Dean of St. Paul's Cathedral. (This is true, so help me God.)
1595	Heels on shoes.
1596	Sir John Harington, English author, designs the first water closet.
1608	Checks appear in the Netherlands. (Check-kiting appears at the same time.)

1630	"Pirates of all nationalities, called 'buccaneers,' settle in Tortuga, off northwest Coast of Hispaniola."* (Calling all pirates!)
1630	Sir John Suckling, an English poet, invents cribbage.
1630	Advertising industry begins in Paris. (1630, a watershed year.)
1643	Parisians go wild over coffee.
1650	First coffeehouse opens in England at Oxford (a college town).
1650	First tea-drinking in England. (Tea eventually wins.)
1653	Finally we get mailboxes—in Paris.
1670	Minute hands on watches.
1677	Parisians go wild over ice cream. (But ice-cream sodas were invented in Philly in 1874 —inexplicably not in the book.)†
1713	Prussian army adopts pigtails. (What can you say?)
1727	Coffee first planted in Brazil. (In 1928, "Brazil's economy collapses owing to over-production of coffee.")‡
1756	Germany's first chocolate factory opens.
1764	House numbers introduced in London.
1852	Los Angeles becomes a city. The beginning of the modern era.

* *The Timetables of History.*
† Ice cream originated in China and Italy (also not in book).
‡ *The Timetables of History.*

How to Recognize the
◆ Stars and Constellations ◆
in the Northern Latitudes

Let's face it, there exists:

The Law of Constellations: No matter how many times you gaze at the night sky or look in constellation books or have a constellation expert explain where the various configurations are that you should memorize—after all this, you know only:
1. the BIG DIPPER,
2. the LITTLE DIPPER or CASSIOPEIA (rarely both), and
3. ORION (often only his belt—how would you like it if they remembered you only for your *belt?*)

It is amazing how alike we all are. It doesn't matter that stars are *the* most important physical items in the universe. Yet even more devastating is **The Law of Stars:** The only star you are certain of (if any) is **Polaris** (the North Star).

The magnificent array of stars that we call "the heavens" rises in the east and sets in the west, (apparently) rotating around *Polaris*, the Pole Star, which remains stationary in its Northern position. A few constellations near Polaris never set*—like the BIG DIPPER, the LITTLE DIPPER, and CASSIOPEIA—and thus are visible all year round, and so are the brilliant stars **Vega** and **Capella,** which are rela-

* These are called "circumpolar" constellations.

tively close to Polaris. Most constellations dip below the horizon for certain periods; some are seen only in the Southern latitudes.

Refer to the sky map (pg. 51) for a picture of the stars and constellations as they are mentioned below. And, removed from city lights, prepare to "heighten" your romantic life.

—— *How to Do It—All Year Round* ——

1. Locate the BIG DIPPER.* We're going to use the stars in its bowl as "pointers" to identify other constellations. We "name" these stars 1, 2, 3, and 4.

2. Use the 2/1 pointer to arrive at Polaris—at the end of the LITTLE DIPPER's handle. In the sky, trace the LITTLE DIPPER.

3. Locate CASSIOPEIA (kas-i-o-*pe*-ya)—five stars that make a "W." It is opposite the BIG DIPPER on the other side of Polaris along the 4/Polaris pointer.

—— *Winter*—The *Best Time for Stars* ——

The Winter Hexagon—a Sky Crystal of Stars: Each star in the Hexagon is actually in a different constellation, and we will identify all of them and four of the constellations: CHARIOTEER, GEMINI, ORION, and TAURUS.

1. Using the 4/1 pointer, locate *Capella* in CHAR- IOTEER, the fourth brightest star in the Northern sky.

2. Using the 4/2 pointer, locate *Pollux* (*Castor*, his mortal twin, is alongside) in GEMINI.

---

* The Big Dipper is not considered an "official" constellation, but a part of a larger one, the Great Bear (Ursa Major). Perhaps we should explain this to billions of human beings, past and present, who have gazed upward just to locate the Big Dipper.

3. Continue on the same pointer until you come to *Sirius*, the "dog-star,"* the most brilliant star in the sky. *Procyon* (*pro*-si-on) means "[rising] before the dog" and is between Pollux and Sirius, to complete one side of the Hexagon.

4. Up from Sirius, locate *Rigel* (rī-j'l), the right foot of ORION (the Hunter). ORION is the most impressive constellation of all. The MILKY WAY runs through its "club." Trace the constellation (refer to the sky map).

5. Continue around toward *Capella* to *Aldebaran* (al-*deb*-e-ran), an orangeish star in the eye of TAURUS, to complete the hexagon.

6. ORION's left shoulder, *Betelgeuse* (*bet*-el-jooz), resides *within* the Hexagon. This reddish "super-giant" is sixteen hundred times larger than our sun.

The Winter Hexagon is quite a display, but in late spring or summer only Capella is generally visible.

7. Locate the *Pleiades*, a "star-cluster" composed of hundreds of stars, only about six of which you can see with your naked eye. It is near Aldebaran on the side away from Betelgeuse.

--------------------- *Summer* ---------------------

The Summer Triangle—the Navigator's Friend:

1. Locate *Deneb* (in the graceful SWAN) by pointing along 3/4 from the BIG DIPPER.

2. Locate *Vega*, the bright star in the constellation next to Deneb. Vega is the right-angle *Vertex* of the Summer Triangle. It's the third brightest star in the Northern sky (Sirius and Arcturus are first and second).

---

* In Canis Major (Greater Dog). The entire constellation is rarely discernible in Northern latitudes.

3. From Deneb move opposite from CASSIOPEIA to locate *Altair* in EAGLE. This completes the (very large) Summer Triangle. The EAGLE is a splendid constellation that has three stars in a line like ORION—don't confuse them.

Navigators can see the Triangle's bright stars during twilight and thus take helpful sightings on the still-visible horizon.

Go get a book on stars—and use the binoculars you got for looking at birds. Check out the spring and autumn stars. Find a **galaxy,** the most distant object you can see with the naked eye, two hundred light-years away and containing more than 2 billion suns!*

> **The Law of Unbelievability:** Over time, even constellations change.

The Pole star *changes*. In twelve thousand years it will be the brilliant Vega—which should make personal flying at night a lot easier.

You will also learn about the **planets**—much too erratic to include on a star map, yet along with the sun and the moon, they move entirely within a thin band called the "ecliptic," inhabited by the zodiac constellations.

Venus we know as both morning and evening star, outshining all but the sun and moon. And some people don't realize that Mars and especially Jupiter, and even Saturn and Mercury, can appear very prominently in the sky.

* The Andromeda Nebula.

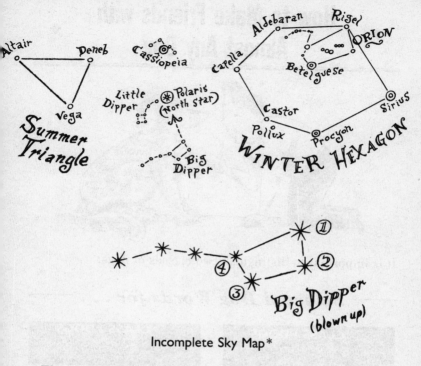

Incomplete Sky Map*

The weirdest thing happens when you start getting engaged with stars. You start—now, this seems crazy but I'll go on anyway—you start *to fall in love with stars.*

* We are using a crucial technical breakthrough, which is described in a well-known book by H. A. Rey, called *The Stars* (Houghton Mifflin, 1976). The author has managed to depict constellations as really looking like their names. So obvious, yet apparently no one ever did it before—except, as he surmises, a long time ago when they invented constellations. I'm surprised that most of the recent—and in general —marvelous books about the sky have not gotten this clearly excellent (and probably historically more accurate) hint.

How to Make Friends with Almost Any Dog

It is important to distinguish two classes of dogs:

Selected Dog Words for . . .

. . . CLASS I DOGS	. . . CLASS 2 DOGS
rrorr, rrorr	grrrr . . . *
wrowr, wrowr	rrrrr . . . *
erruf, erruf	
woof (English Sheep Dog)	
hwrohwr, hwrohwr	
etc.	

CLASS 1
Almost any dog.

* Especially if muttered.

CLASS 2

Dogs that make Class 2 sounds; dogs that retract their lips and bare their teeth while making Class 2 sounds; dogs who do all of the above plus are crouched to spring. Class 2 dogs include attack dogs, callously neglected animals, or those whose job is to guard Hell. Class 2 dogs are quite rare, and besides, we're not going to address them here.

The Problem

I assume that you are a person that a dog—or dogs—bark at, ignore, or fall asleep in front of. Or maybe you're about to meet your friend's dog for the first time, and even though you know this dog is "okay," (i.e., Class 1), you're afraid.

How to Do It

1. **Remove your knapsack and put down any heavy equipment.** To some dogs, you are what you look like; i.e., they see your apparent shape as you.

So if you are a mailperson, a refrigerator delivery person, an *ice person*, or are just carrying a large package, a dog may perceive that you have *a weird and unfamiliar-looking body*. This may give the dog the right to intimidate you and, well, argue with you.

2. **To gain a dog's attention, *talk slowly and calmly*.** Don't raise your voice (that's for reprimands and emergencies). No matter how large the dog is, imagine that it's like a small child, or a puppy learning English. Try to relax and move slowly. One expert observes that the word *what* has an almost magical effect on a dog—as in "What a good dog!"* I agree.

---

* Barbara Woodhouse, *No Bad Dogs*, Summit Books, 1984.

Dogs respect honesty. So it's not enough to blurt out words. *You have to actually talk to the dog.* For real. Many experienced dog people even tell you to talk "baby talk." This works, too, and it helps to know why.

Children can pull on a dog's body parts, ride a dog (euphemism for torturing a dog), slobber on a dog, etc., and the dog generally puts up with it. Why?

A dog knows these are kids and kids are innocent like puppies and kids like to be "doggy" with them and dogs appreciate that. When you talk baby talk, you get *doggier.*

Well, then, why not just get down on all fours and bark and so on? No. It is not a good idea to try to turn into a dog, since the dog then perceives you as a competitive threat, or a sexual object, and may try to drive you away (or do some other things). The knack is to be genuinely doggy without turning into an actual dog, which is also dishonest unless you really are a dog.

Another reason that dogs often (not always) put up with children is that dogs find people, especially adult people, mostly boring. Though they are genuinely fond of us and love us—and they also know where their next meal is coming from—in their view, we're completely predictable. But kids aren't as predictable and dogs like to play with them.

3. If you want to make an impression on a dog who is ignoring you, *do something unusual.* Ease into an infrequent posture (imitate a French mime? stand on your head?), or make soft, funny sounds. If none of this works, just ignore the dog.

4. Stand your ground. Unless the dog is so friendly that it's hostile, jumping all over you, try not to back away. Just "stay" and be patient. The dog may then come over to check you out. There's nothing to fear. It's a Class 1 dog. Sooner or later you'll have to relate to this. Why not now?

5. Don't extend your hand too far. This is not because the dog will bite, but because he may take that as a sign of weakness or fear. It's better to open your hand, keeping it reasonably close to your body. The dog may come over, sniff it, and then lick it. Then you're in love and everything's okay.

6. If you really can't control your fear, then sit down (on the floor if you can't find a chair).

7. Do not put your grimy, or nongrimy, paws all over an unfamiliar dog to "pet" him. This is not necessarily a good thing for the dog, unless the dog asks for it.

More than one dog lover claims that a most effective way to make contact with a dog is to touch it on the chest. On the other hand, I have to caution you. If you just go up and thwop any dog any old way on the chest, that dog might consider you someone who bears watching. It all depends on how you do it. A dog's chest is a sensitive area. Standing to the side, you can try touching the dog there as if you are passing a secret that only the two of you know.

Please remember that you're making a friend.

◆ How to Fix a Leaky Faucet ◆

Dispelling the Fear of Endless Gushing Water—i.e., fixing that annoying (and wasteful) *dripping faucet* that you used to pay to have the plumber do—is amazingly easy (otherwise it wouldn't be in my book). But repairing a leaky faucet is the archetype how-to-do-it activity—and this is not supposed to be a regular how-to-do-it book! However, we don't stand on ceremony here, so let's get straight to it:

If you can collect together **a screwdriver, an adjustable wrench, pliers, a clean rag** (to be used with the wrench to avoid scratches), **and maybe some household oil** (like WD-40), you can fix a leaky faucet.

1. Turn off the water from under the sink (those two little knobs on the pipes leading up to the faucet) —or at the main, where it comes into your house.

2. Turn on the faucet and let the remaining water run out. Now plug up the drain (or use a cloth) so various small screws won't wash down and feed alligators in the sewers.

3. Remove the faucet handle. ◄ Do not bang anything. ► To remove the handle, look for a screw—you may first have to pry off a decorative cap with a nonvaluable knife —or remove a nut. Use a drop of oil if it sticks. The handle will then come off, but if there are any little pieces (like a washer), save them because they go back on later.

4. Unscrew the obvious nut. (When you get the handle off, there *will* be an obvious nut.) Use the wrench (with the rag), finish unscrewing by hand, and lift it up and out.

5. Remove the *assembly* below. Either lift it out (jiggling it a little, if necessary) or unscrew it (in this case, unscrew in the ON direction).* If you have trouble un-

* This, of course, is the opposite of the usual direction. (See "Directions for Screwing," pg. 186.)

screwing it, the clever way is to put the handle back on and use the extra leverage it provides. Once it is unscrewed, you will see the ailing *washer* that caused all the trouble screwed in to the underside of the assembly.

 Washer with Screw   Packing Nut

6. Remove the screw that holds the washer. You can use pliers if it's all rusted and crumbly. If the washer is beveled,* then *notice which way it was set in*. Should there be some other weird-looking object instead of the normal-looking washer, then replace *that*.

7. Obtain a washer that's *exactly* the same type and size—and get another screw. (You've either bought these earlier using the model of your sink as a reference, or you will take the washer and screw with you to the plumber supply or hardware store.)

8. Apply The Great Law of Undoing by putting everything back in reverse. Remember to insert the new washer the correct way.

— *Optional Thought and Nonthought* —

Think about the fact that you do three or more things every day that are more complicated than undoing and putting back a faucet assemblage.

Do not think about all the money you've spent in the past to have someone else come and fix a drip.

---

* Mechanic's talk for a sloping surface or edge.

How to Find Out Even the Seemingly Impossible

Apple seller: You sound like you're the first lad who ever saw an apple fall down.
Newton: You don't understand. The apple fell down.
Apple seller: Boy, are you dumb. How else would an apple fall?

The Science of Finding Out is extremely important. It is actually an exercise of the imagination.

How to Do It

First, you must need this information. The more you need it, the easier you'll get it. Your need will affect not only your ability to persevere and to take strangely bold (and courteous) leaps, it will even permeate your *voice* in a non-hysterical way.

- Test Case—The Law of Calling Yale -

Your colleague has called and said that she needs to know right away if a certain moderately well-known person attended Yale University. Could you find out?

1. You phone a *suburban* library (librarians there may have more time). You ask if the person is listed in *Who's Who* (or *Who Was Who*, if the subject has departed). No entry.

2. Impelled by the urgency of the situation, you take a leap of the imagination: You call Yale directly. But wait! What will you say? And to whom?

3. The Alumni Association! The library is always a backup, in this case the Yale Library. It may be obvious, but the library is your universal rescuer—and usually for isolated facts you can use the telephone. Librarians are modern heroes—unprejudiced, persevering, courteous, and skilled. They also have amazing secret sources.

4. Universal rescuers include libraries, librarians, telephone books, and information operators. For instance, "What's the weather like there in Cheyenne?" or "Where is the best place in Vermont (or Canada) to order maple syrup?" (After midnight, information operators mostly welcome a chance to chat and help out.) Of course, you will discover your own personal rescuers. For instance, the concierge in a fine hotel can give you restaurant tips.

Optional

Speaking of the phone company—or any large utility—suppose you are trying to get some information or help, say with a bill or other problem. You're getting nowhere with the service person, who, in your opinion, is officious, unsympathetic, angry, whatever. And you begin, for the 403rd time, your traditional large-utility-company curse (by now there is a gene that carries this curse).

Forget all that. *Hang up, call right back, and get someone else.* What you want is a courteous rebel, who enjoys working around the organization to actually help a customer. This person will not only understand your problem, but will assist you even if it means harmlessly bending a rule. (Don't abuse this method; use it only in an "emergency.")

Nothing bad will happen if you hang up. I know it's rude, but you can say (in your cheeriest voice) the ironic truth: "Sorry, it's an emergency. I'll call back later." (Click.)

Imagination and the Science of Finding Out

For some reason, it seems to take a certain imagination to imagine something that is actually "self-evident" (for example, _The Law of Gravity_). Often, though, to take action you need a kind of reverse imagination—e.g., to _not_ imagine that something irrational will happen (your gas will be disconnected because you hung up on a representative, you will be cited as a pest in the Yale newspaper, and so on).

By the way, even after the computers appear to take over our information chores, there will always be a need to understand _The Law of Calling Yale_.

◆ How to Build a Fire ◆

One of the remarkable deficiencies in modern civilized life is that there are large numbers of intelligent—even brilliant —human beings who don't know how to build consistently good fires in their fireplaces.

Why single out fire building? Well, after ten, maybe fifty, or even one hundred _thousand_ years of practice, you would assume that by this time we would all possess a _fire-building gene_. If we do, it seems that there is also a _fire-stupid gene_ working hard to cancel it.

Preparation

Check the Damper. Make sure it's open. (However, to prevent heat loss, close the damper when not in use.)

Tools. Poker, tongs, broom, shovel (or dustpan).

Wood. Dry hardwood is the best: more heat, longer fire —and don't throw out those highly burnable charcoal fragments from your previous fire. Ash, oak, hard maple, hickory, or birch are excellent.

Kindling. Softwood is the choice, which is usually an evergreen such as pine, cedar, or fir.

PRELIMINARIES

A couple of inches of ash underneath is actually helpful for keeping the fire hot, since the ash reduces the amount of heat absorbed by the hearth. But if there's too much build-up, sweep it up.

There are basically two kinds of fires: *roaring* and *comfortable*. No one needs an explanation for the joy of roaring fires. However, this type of fire sometimes sends much of its heat up the chimney. Of course, if you're sitting right in front of the flames, you will always be warm (at least in front).

If you want to convey as much heat as possible into the room, then consider building a comfortable fire. This is less dramatic, but it produces more usable heat.

The Roaring—or Quasi-Roaring—Fire

1. Crumple single newspaper pages. ◄ To make them burn longer, roll or twist the pages tightly. Take the time to prepare. ► And never use colored paper (chemicals).

2. On top of the paper, crisscross a lot of split kin-

61

dling so it won't fall through. On top of the kindling, set three logs—two on the bottom and one on top in between the bottom two—so that all three logs are parallel to the opening.

3. For faster lighting, face the split, or flat, side of the logs downward since that side burns more easily. Leave enough room between logs for the air to circulate.

4. Tend the fire. For example, you may wish to eventually turn the bottom logs so that their undersides (which have been cooking the most) are now facing you. The top log may then drop down and you can put another log on top. Adding additional logs may increase "roaringness."

The Comfortable Fire

The reflecting type fire was also employed before the dawn of history.

1. Place a large-diameter log at the rear of the hearth. This not only reflects the heat outward, but decreases the size of the opening, which brings the heat closer to the room.

2. Now simply build any kind of decent fire in front of this thicker log, using three smaller-diameter logs. One good way is to use a top-most log with at least one split side. Straddle the split side between the side of the large log and the top of the smaller one that's down in front of it, so that the split side faces back and slightly down.

Tricks

If an imperfect chimney design makes it hard to start a fire and speed its development (without smoking up the room):

1. **Curl up a sheet of newspaper, light one end, and hold it up into the flue for a few moments until the flame begins to "draw" upward.** Then use the paper to light the fire.

If smoke should waft into the room:

2. **Try opening up a window, which creates a stronger updraft in the chimney.**

Above All, Experiment

The movement of heat is not so simple. As essential as warmth and fire has been to humans since before the caves, we had to wait until the *eighteenth century* before we obtained the correct principles of fireplace heating—and it took brilliant scientists like Benjamin Franklin and Count Rumford (who also invented baking powder) to do it.

Recommended

You may think I'm a crazy daredevil, but if the fire doesn't spark, *and you are there watching it the whole time*, you can remove the screen, since it holds back much of the heat. Not only is this safe, it is recommended if you wish to realize the full measure of satisfaction from your fire—whether comfortable, quasi-roaring, or one with large, gnarled, primeval logs and vast, roaring flames.

Optional, Unless You're Faced with this Situation

The heat doesn't work and you are out of logs. The only flammable furniture consists of those "antique" chairs bestowed on you by your Aunt Boris. (If you have an aunt named Boris, then you have chairs like this.) What do you do? Who can save you?

The *New York Sunday Times!* (Or a surrogate.) Stack up several open sheets of its (endless) number of pages. Starting at one corner, tightly roll up the pile, working diagonally across to the other corner. Twist the roll. Continue this way until the entire ex-newspaper is transformed. "Smart" logs —that last! (If you're out of kindling, tie a *knot* in each roll instead of twisting.)

You have just employed a variation of:

> **The Law of Newspapers:** Without newspapers, modern people would be almost helpless since nobody could pack anything for mailing, clean up spills, or train dogs.

◆ How to Flip Pancakes and Other Flippables ◆

Look at that world-class chef—you!—flip those things! (Omelets, pancakes, vegetables, whatever.) Flipping not only looks good, but is supposed to be good for the food.

—— *How to Do It* ——

1. Start by "virtual flipping." I.e., practice flipping something uncooked in a cold pan—like a piece of bread. (If it drops on the floor, so what?) The pan should be large enough to easily accommodate the food, but not so heavy that you can't manipulate it. A pan with sloping sides is best.

2. Start with the pan about waist high and raise it DIAGONALLY UP AND AWAY FROM YOU, applying a little scooping motion so that the pan ends up coming back in toward you, somewhat *above* your waist. Don't try to do funny extra things with your wrist. If you follow these instructions, flipping takes place automatically.

At first, exaggerate the movement described. The expression "You've got it down" applies here. It means you can downsize your movement, which makes it appear more modest. When you begin flipping with "real" food, there will naturally be some differences—for instance, between flipping pancakes and a pan full of zucchini. But that's all part of the fun.

3. Try flipping with an assortment of pans. You will very quickly find out why a pan with sloping sides is easier to work with, why it needs to be large enough relative to the flippables, and why it shouldn't be too heavy for you. This knowledge cannot adequately be passed on from a book.

Optional Query

Why didn't those (otherwise excellent) cookbooks tell us how to do this?*

---

* I wrote a cookbook myself and I didn't tell the reader how to do this and I am embarrassed. *The Fear of Cooking*, Houghton Mifflin, 1984, pg. nothing.

How to Send Food Back in a Restaurant

Ignus and his brilliant but modest companion Mango are having dinner in a restaurant. Ignus is known both for his willingness to make mistakes and his willingness to repeat them. How did he get this way? One might say that two roads diverged in a wood—more precisely, in a woodsy suburban area—and Ignus took both of them.

Ignus says that something seems wrong with his food.

Mango replies, "Then you have to send it back. Call the waiter over and have him take it back."

Ignus signals the waiter, somewhat tentatively. The waiter is extremely professional looking, challenging him with piercing eyes that disclose to all that this diner is on the lowest possible rung of any ladder you could think up.

"Uh, have you ever eaten this fish?"

"I wouldn't dream of eating that fish," the waiter replies.

"You wouldn't?"

"No."

"But . . . but this is a seafood restaurant!" (He points to the sign over the door, which says, THE GALLOPING FISH.)

"What?!" the waiter exclaims. He thrusts off his apron with a large blowfish on it and pulls out of his (large) pocket, and ties on, another apron that has a cow eating flowers. Our hero looks up at the sign. It now reads, THE RELENTLESS COW. The waiter has gone off to another table.

Mango says, "You have to be more firm."

"More firm, yes." He calls the waiter over again. The waiter's expression is opaque.

"This food stinks. It's totally disgusting." The waiter opens his mouth in astonishment, then begins to cry, and then to bawl. The restaurant help and the patrons, casting looks of contempt on the insensitivity of the baffled diner, console the waiter, and escort him off as the tears continue to roll.

Mango quietly calls out, "Waiter." The waiter reappears with an impassive demeanor and now sports an apron emblazoned with a huge celery stalk.

Mango nods toward Ignus's plate. "There's something wrong with this. Please take it back."

The waiter kisses her on both cheeks and removes the food. All the waiters applaud. All the waiters in all other restaurants applaud. So do the people in all other restaurants' *paintings*. Of course, we may never know if Ignus actually got the message.

But we did.

◆ How to Understand Football ◆

Huge (generally good-natured) people are enmeshed in a struggle that (1) entertains a large segment of the world's population, (2) redistributes wealth wholesale, and (3) is a really bizarre activity when you come to think about it (it's better than war, okay?).

The Game of Football in Brief

The field is 100 yards long with a *goal line* at each end plus a 10-yard *end zone* beyond. Playing time is 30 minutes for each half. Each team has 11 players on the field, and at any given time one team is on *offense*; the other, *defense*.

AIM

The offense tries to score and can "block" the defensive players. The offense has "possession" of the ball and has four plays to move as far as possible toward the opponents' goal line (or end zone). **A team moves forward when an eligible runner runs with the ball, or an eligible receiver catches a pass and continues to run—until he is "tackled,"* goes out of bounds, fumbles, or scores.** The defense tries to tackle the offensive ball-carrier or run him out of bounds. If the defense should recover a fumble (i.e., fall on top of it) or intercept a pass, it gets to go on offense.

DOWNS

At the end of each down, or play, the ball is placed on the *line of scrimmage*, which is where the offense's forward motion was just stopped. Whenever the offense moves *10 yards or more* within four downs, it gets a *first down* from the new line of scrimmage. Beginning with any first down, if the offense fails to move at least 10 yards in four plays (downs), the defense "gets the ball" and becomes the offense.

The offense continues until they either lose possession of the ball or score a *touchdown* or *field goal*. You now know the basic rules.

PUNTING

On the fourth down, the offense must decide whether to go for a first down or to punt (kick) the ball, forcing the defense back. If the offense tries to make a first down and is unsuccessful, then the defense gets to take possession at the line of scrimmage. Usually, the offense punts.

FORWARD PASS

(Or simply a *pass*.) Must be thrown before the passer advances beyond the line of scrimmage.

---

* Only a player in possession of the ball can be tackled.

SCORING

The offense can score a *touchdown* (6 points) by running or passing the ball into the opponent's end zone.

After each touchdown, the offense can score *an extra point* by place-kicking the ball from the 2-yard line through the uprights. A team scores 2 extra points if it chooses to run or pass.

During regular play, the offense can score a *field goal* (3 points) by place-kicking the ball through the uprights.

The defense can score 2 points on a *safety*, but this is so rare we'll leave it for independent study.

THE TOUCHBACK

The offense may catch a punt or a kick-off, and the defense may intercept a pass, in their own respective end zones, and opt for a *touchback* by touching the ball to the ground (or "downing" it). You would also do this if monsters were approaching you at the speed of light (even if you were a monster). The ball is placed on the 20-yard line with *no score* tallied.

The Players

THE OFFENSIVE LINE (SEVEN LINEMEN)
End, tackle, guard, center, guard, tackle, end.

THE OFFENSIVE BACKFIELD (FOUR BACKS)
Quarterback (QB) and three other backs. In general, the backs line up as running or blocking backs (though they can also catch passes), or as wide receivers, more obviously positioned for the thrill of catching a (possibly very long) pass. Depending on the *offensive formation*, backs have different names. Two common designations are *fullback* (some-

one bigger and stronger than you) and *halfback* (someone surprisingly light and fast who will beat you in leg or arm wrestling). By the way, just before the ball is snapped, various offensive backs may seem to be jogging back and forth to get exercise—actually it's part of "football deception."

ELIGIBILITY
Any back can receive the ball on the "snap" from the center and run with it or pass. Generally the QB takes the snap and either hands the ball off to another back, or passes it to an eligible receiver, or runs with it himself. There are *five* eligible pass receivers: three backs and two ends.

THE DEFENSIVE LINE
Commonly end, tackle, tackle, end—with three linebackers behind the line, backing them up. This is a "4-3 defense." There are many other possibilities.

THE DEFENSIVE BACKFIELD, OR "SECONDARY"
Often four backs: cornerback, free safety (who is free to range about), strong safety (who lines up opposite the offensive tight end), and cornerback.

A Football Glossary for the Sunday Fan

Even though you've been watching and listening to NFL games for years—and you may have even played football in high school—in spite of all the time invested, there are terms that are still fuzzy in your mind. This glossary includes some of the most basic football words an *announcer* might use, and may contain that one clarification, or two, that have always eluded you.

Audible. A play that the QB changes just before the ball is snapped—after a (split-second) survey of the defensive formation.

Blitz. A safety—or a linebacker—comes hurtling through the line toward the QB as soon as the ball is snapped.

Bootleg. The QB hides the ball against his hip—after faking a hand-off to a running back—then runs, laterals, or passes it.

Down lineman. A defensive lineman.

Draw play. The QB moves back pretending to pass, which "draws" the defense—he then hands it off to another back, who runs through the gap in the defense, or else the QB keeps it.

Field goal distance. Add 17 yards to the line of scrimmage.

Flanker back. See wide receiver.

Flea-flicker. The QB hands off to a back, who laterals back to the QB, who then passes.

Free safety. A middle defensive back who lines up on the opposite side from the *strong safety.*

Hail Mary. In football, a symbolic term suggesting that all religions have beings in charge of hopeless but sincere desires; specifically, a long, last-second, desperation pass is launched to a receiver who is generally surrounded by hordes of defenders—and "miraculously" wins the game. (Sometimes it actually does.)

Nickel defense. A defensive alignment employing five backs.

Overtime. An extra quarter (fifteen minutes) if game ends in a tie; scoring is by "sudden death"—during regular season there is only one overtime.

Pitchout. A lateral behind the line of scrimmage.

Play-action pass or play-fake. The QB fakes a hand-off, then drops back to pass.

Pocket. The area around the QB where his blockers protect him on passing plays.

Run and shoot offense. A play that requires the QB, while calling signals, to also call out options—e.g., whether it will be a run or pass play—after he surveys the defensive line-up.

Sack. The QB is tackled behind the line of scrimmage.

Screen pass. The offensive line lets the defense penetrate, then the QB throws over the defender's heads.

Secondary. The defensive backfield.

Setback. The lone offensive running back in a type of "I" formation.

Shotgun. An offensive (usually passing) formation where the QB gets the snap five yards back from the center, and is an eligible receiver.

Slotback. In an "I" formation, an offensive back who lines up just behind the line of scrimmage in the slot between the tackle and split end.

Split end. See wide receiver.

Strong safety. A middle defensive back who lines up across from the (offensive) tight end.

Strong side. The more compact side of the offensive line; the tight end lines up on this side.

Swing pass. Pass thrown to a receiver moving nearly horizontal to the line of scrimmage.

Tailback. In an "I" formation, an offensive back who lines up farthest to the rear.

Tight end. Lines up "tight" with the tackle and not only catches passes but blocks linemen on running plays.

Weak side. The less compact side of the offensive line; the split end lines up on this side.

Wide out. A wide receiver.

Wide receiver. Also called a *flanker back* or *split end*—generally a speedster who "splits" off from the line.

Wingback. A running back who lines up near the line of scrimmage just beyond the tight end.

Optional

On Super Bowl Sunday, if you are not watching TV or keeping a fan company, you are free to go for a drive in the country (no cars on the road) or a mysterious walk in the totally silent city (no one is anywhere).

Tips on Fractions, Decimals, ◆ and Percents

Tyler is methodical, obsessively neat, and can do a job in half a day. Morgan is sloppy, obsessed by the big picture, and has a large parrot. He does the same job in one and a half days. How long will it take if they do the job together?

— *Fractions Are Definitely Strange* —

You will never get anywhere with fractions if you complain that they should behave like regular whole numbers. You have to make peace with their weirdness. But lots of things are weird.

Imagine a room whose only occupants are a table and a chair. There are laws involved here: For example, the furniture doesn't move by itself; the room is quiet, serene. Or is it?

The fact is, tables and chairs "don't know it," but they're composed throughout of molecules, and these molecules behave *very differently* from tables and chairs, which is pretty amazing. If the table and chair were to become aware of these molecules (this would be uncanny, but suppose), they would notice, for instance, that molecules are constantly *whizzing around.*

The point of this ridiculous analogy is that just as molecules appear strange to tables and chairs, so do fractions with respect to "whole" numbers (1, 2, 3, etc.). For example, fractions seem to be almost everywhere—in between the whole numbers, above them and below them.* And fractions "move around." For instance, ½ can be ²⁄₄ or ¹³⁄₂₆, or God knows what.

Stark Dread—The Division of Fractions

1. A Fundamental Fact. They lied to you in school when they said fractions consist of only a "numerator" and a "denominator."

> **The Fundamental Law of Fractions:** The "–" that separates the numbers in a fraction means "divided by."

* Actually, like molecules, there's a lot of space between fractions and there are even more strange kinds of numbers that fill up those spaces. They are called, quite appropriately, "irrational numbers." And you bet; they're absolutely nuts. If you think that's picturesque, wait till you hear about *transcendental numbers.* Don't worry, they're not in this book.

2. Since, in a fraction, "–" simply means *divided by*, then, for example, ⅗ means *3 divided by 5*, or ⅕ of 3 (i.e., a "fraction" of 3). Though this fundamental fact may help clarify what fractions are in order to overcome THE DREAD OF THE DIVISION OF FRACTIONS, you need a secret trick called EARS.*

EARS

"EARS" is known by every great mathematician. (I guess at some stage in their careers, it comes in the mail or something.)

Suppose you have to divide ³⁄₁₁ by ⁴⁄₉. From now on, you don't even have to think about how to do this. You recall the Fundamental Fact that "–" means "divided by," and you then construct the following hideous-looking display of four numbers.

$$\frac{\frac{3}{11}}{\frac{4}{9}}$$

To turn this into a decent-looking ordinary fraction, you use EARS:

← ear

Your "EARS" drawing will show that 3 × 9 are placed *together* on top (the numerator) and 4 × 11 remain *together* on the bottom (the denominator). In this case, we have ²⁷⁄₄₄.

If you have a whole number involved, like the "3" in

---

* If the words they drummed into you in school—"to divide two fractions, multiply by the reciprocal"—never worked for you, just relax. Now you have EARS. ("Reciprocal" means that you turn one of the fractions upside-down—the second one, actually—but what if you don't remember?)

3/11/3, you simply turn the 3 into a fraction by putting a 1 in the denominator—$3/1$, giving 3/11/3/1. Using EARS, we have $3 \times 1 / 11 \times 3 = 3/33 = 1/11$.*

We will not cope here with the possibly starker dread of THE ADDITION OF FRACTIONS, except to remind you that to add two or more fractions, you have to make all of their denominators the same. This takes some practice. (English school kids get to learn the following: "You can't add haddock to cod without making fish pie." Unfortunately for them, not liking fish pie is never an authorized excuse for not turning in homework.)

Decimal Strangeness

Anyone who has tried to explain decimals (actually a kind of *fraction*) encounters what appears to be one of the dumbest mistakes ever made during the creation of the world. You would think that whoever was responsible for fabricating numbers would have done something like this:

$$.1 = 1. \text{ (or 1)}$$
$$.01 = 1/10$$
$$.001 = 1/100 \text{ etc.}$$

Very symmetrical. The number of *zeros* on both sides is the same. *But it's wrong.* Instead, this is what came out:

$$.1 = 1/10$$
$$.01 = 1/100$$
$$.001 = 1/1000 \text{ etc.}$$

* If you ask great or famous mathematicians about "EARS," they will either smile knowingly—or else look blank, pretending they've never heard of it. This behavior is bizarre, but great mathematicians work very hard and can be accorded some leeway.

This is right.

1. In a decimal, the number of *digits* on the left equals the number of *zeros* on the right. (It turns out the first way runs into a snag very fast, so the Developers did a really smashing job here.)

Once you recognize that this is what causes your confusion, the confusion will disappear—because THERE IS NOTHING ELSE DIFFICULT ABOUT DECIMALS. They are simply a shorthand translation of an ordinary fraction which has a 1 followed by some zeros in the denominator.

2. To change a fraction into a decimal: Do what the "–" tells you to do—*divide* the numerator by the denominator, which is what a fraction "means." E.g., $\frac{3}{5}$ is 3 (or 3.0) divided by 5, which is .6—because you know how to do basic division.

3. To change a decimal into a fraction is even easier: Consider all the digits to the right of the decimal point, the *numerator*, and the number of these digits tells you how many *zeros* are in the denominator. E.g., .3692 is $\frac{3692}{10,000}$—four digits (3, 6, 9, 2) making up the numerator, and thus there are four *zeroes* in the denominator (10,000).

Percents

There is absolutely nothing the least profound or difficult about percents. They were invented by resourceful merchants to make things easier—like marking up prices.

1. To change a percent into a fraction, *divide by a hundred*. E.g., $80\% = \frac{80}{100} = \frac{4}{5}$. That's what per-cent means: Divide by a hundred. More often, however, one wants to convert an ordinary fraction into a percent.

2. To change a fraction into a percent, *multiply*

the fraction by 100. E.g., ⅘ × 100 = 80, which is 80%.

3. To change a decimal fraction to a percent is even easier. You multiply the decimal by a hundred, so you move the decimal point **two places to the *right*.** E.g., .35 is 35%, and .0035 is .35%.

4. To change a percent to a decimal fraction, you move the decimal point two places to the *left*. This is the same as dividing the decimal by 100 (which is what percent means). So 35% is .35, and .35% is .0035. AND THAT'S PERCENTS.

How to Change a Fuse, ◆ or Fear of Suicide ◆

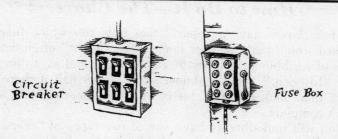

Circuit Breaker

Fuse Box

You can do this even if you don't have any idea what electricity is. The truth is nobody really knows what electricity is.

If you ask a regular good teacher or scientist, they'll say something like "The author who told you that doesn't know what he's talking about.* Electricity is . . . blah, blah,

---

* This is true because I don't know what electricity is.

79

blah . . ." And you still don't know what it is.

But ask a scientist of the first rank and he or she will probably say something like "The truth is nobody really knows what electricity is." Take it from me, don't worry.

—— *How to Do It—General Advice* ——

Take a flashlight with you to the fuse box. And don't be the least put off by the following cautionary comment—it's traditional and sensible, even though many people who change fuses fearlessly are unaware of it:

CAUTIONARY COMMENT: *While doing this utterly simple job, don't stand on a wet surface* (but it's a rare home that's wet where the fuse box is), and don't grasp a metal object with your other hand. Use one hand and leave the other hand at your side—or in your pocket. Okay, that's that.

—— *How to Do It—The Chart* ——

All fuse boxes have a "chart" that tells you which fuses govern which parts of your home. This "chart" often consists of scribblings on ratty pieces of paper and says things like "Kitchen," "Hall" (almost never *which* hall if there's more than one), etc. But this is what the ancestors left, so don't complain.

You will undoubtedly have one of two types of "fuses": (1) circuit breakers, which look like light switches, or (2) "regular" fuses, which look like fuses.

—— *How to Do It—If You Have* —— *Circuit Breakers*

This is the easiest because they don't have to be replaced.

These are simply switches, like light switches, that flip to the "off" position when the circuit is overloaded.

1. Look at the "chart" to verify which breaker flipped off, and switch it back on. (There may be other breakers set to "off" that aren't being used.)

_____ *How to Do It—If You Have* _____ *"Regular" Fuses*

1. Shut off the main switch. With regular fuses, it's usually either a lever or handle that you pull down, or "cartridge blocks" that you pull out by the handle. (Make sure you turn on your flashlight before you do this—the main switch controls the lights in the fuse box room too!)

2. Look at the "chart" to see which fuse blew. Occasionally there are two fuses covering the same part of the house. Though you can employ trial and error, an easier way is to examine the center of the fuse. If you see a metal strip with an obvious break in it, or if it has a burnt-out smudge, you're looking at a blown fuse.

3. Unscrew the fuse—counterclockwise. It's usually easy to unscrew, and it's a totally safe procedure.

4. Look at the *number* on the fuse and replace it with a fuse that has the *same number* on it. It will say 15 or 20 or something with an "A" after the number (the "A" stands for *amperes*—do you really want to know what that is?). **CAUTION:** *Never use a replacement that has a higher number on it.*

5. Turn the main switch back on.

6. Test. Is everything working again? If not, be sure you changed the right fuse.

This whole procedure is one iota more complicated than changing a light bulb.

You can plug a radio, with the volume turned up, into the circuit you're trying to revive. When you replace the correct fuse, you'll hear it. You won't have to go back to check.

How to Get Up
◆ in the Morning, and ◆
Its Importance

"Only dull people are brilliant at breakfast."
Oscar Wilde, An Ideal Husband

Preparation

Trouble getting up in the morning may be due to lack of sound sleep. The following advice can help correct this.

1. Eat supper earlier. (And note that "red" meat takes longer to fully digest than fowl or fish.) Some people can actually wake up in the middle of the night, eat a big meal, and go back to sleep. Others can't eat within three or four hours of going to bed. There are lots of books that tell you what to do about every which thing, but they don't always take into account that people aren't all the same.

2. Picture a nice day coming. For instance: You have to be up at four in the morning because you're flying to Paris. Getting up? No problem, as you bound out of bed.

3. Be physically tired before retiring. Before going to bed, take a walk or do a chore and/or some exercises (sex counts). But if, after this, you engage in *mental work*, you're back where you started.

Waking-Up Machinery

The technology of waking up is overdeveloped. Though there are certainly cases where a mechanism is required to help with breathing, walking, eating, etc., these are activities that people should, if possible, perform on their own. *But some people were never advised that they were designed to wake up as easily as any other animal.* However, to accomplish this in our present overcivilized condition, it may be necessary to retrain. This takes approximately one week and costs no money.

1. Eliminate the snooze alarm. (There are genuine exceptional circumstances, but they are so rare we won't discuss them.) A moment's serious thought will disclose the utter absurdity of this gadget, which has been marketed aggressively to take advantage of our desire to have a piece of candy before we've done anything at all. Nothing the least puritanical is involved in forgoing this cushy devise. You will simply arise with more zip and zest for life.

2. Get up almost immediately. Let's not flagellate ourselves. When the alarm goes off—or your own internal alarm, which everyone mysteriously possesses*—take a moment of quiet, to stretch if that is your wont, and then without haste remove the covers and arise out of bed.

◄ In the beginning this may be one of the most difficult projects you have ever undertaken. ► Nevertheless, almost

* No one knows how this operates.

every human being *can* do this. (It's not illegal for a spouse or lover to help.) Practice this for a week and you will come up against the *addiction* of mushing in bed for no reason. Trust that once you're up, you'll feel great.

NOTE: This doesn't mean you should never sleep late. We're addressing only the wishy-washiness of returning to sleep after the alarm goes off.

3. If you're wide awake before you think you're supposed to get up, get up immediately. If you have the courage to try this, you may be surprised to find that you don't need any more sleep that day, and in fact you feel terrific. Furthermore, if this happens to you and you go back to sleep, sometimes you might actually wake up more tired.

NOTE: People usually need less sleep in summer than in winter. Also, we seem to need less sleep as we get older. But you will never find out how much sleep *you* need unless you *experiment*.

——— *The Importance of Being Up* ———

The following are just some of the activities that are difficult to accomplish while asleep: loving, working, playing, remembering, and shopping.

◆ Aiming a Hammer—The Art of ◆ Not Aiming

Hammering and sawing are the symbolic fundamental carpentry skills. Have you ever seen a generic picture of a

carpenter featuring a screwdriver? Some of us may never need to hammer, but this is such a basic part of our civilization and, more important, of our personal education, that I have included an expanded treatment.

Hammering is an important skill. In learning to hammer, you will encounter in a natural way the omnipresent *Law of Before*.

The Law of Before: The *collecting movement* is the true beginning of an action, though the releasing movement takes all the credit.

This Law operates in almost every facet of your life, such as kicking, swinging a golf club, scything, sweeping, and even playing the piano. The best way to become intimately familiar with this Law is to practice applying it in specific situations. For instance, hammering.

—— *For Those Who Already Know* ——

Before you knew how to hammer properly, you thought (I'll bet) something like this: "I may not be able to hit a nail hard enough—or I may not even be able to hit a nail at all—but nobody has to tell me how to *swing*. I mean you just pick up the hammer and whack it down on that nail. You do it enough times and pretty soon you're *swinging a hammer!*"

Then you found out how wrong that was. And fortunately most everybody finds out before they sprain their arms (or worse), because some kind, or exasperated, older being shows us how.

—— *How to Do It—Before Doing It* ——

The right way is contrary to the naive approach. The key to successful hammering is mostly in the *upstroke*, and that's why The Law of Before applies. There's actually no stop between the upstroke and the downstroke. It may look like a stop, but you should sense no discontinuity.

One often hears older beings say, "Let the weight of the hammer carry it down." Though this is not quite precise, that's the way it feels when you're doing it right. The weight provides most of the raw power, while your body, through your hand, arm, and shoulder, acts as a fulcrum to give the tool an extra oomph of momentum on the way down. The idea is to do this without jerking—never push the hammer down on the target.

Then how do you guide the hammer to its destination?

You don't have to—really. I mean suppose you're walking along and there's a little puddle in front of you. Do you have to "aim" in order to skip over it and not get wet? Of course not. If you apply The Law of Before and just try to swing the hammer the way we're talking about here, "aiming" takes care of itself. Yes, it's remarkable. But so are hundreds of other activities you perform every day.

At first you're afraid that you won't hit the nail—and maybe you won't. But after a while you'll find that you're much more accurate. Working this way, hammering is not only very satisfying, but much less fatiguing. You could hammer all day. It's a good example of how to apply force without violence.

How to Do It—While Doing It

1. Hold the hammer near the handle's end for a full swing.

2. Hold the nail between the thumb and index finger of your nonhammering hand.

3. Tap the nail *lightly* until it stands up in the wood by itself.

4. Remove your fingers from the battlefield.

5a. Drive the nail into the wood using moderate force, with each stroke slightly stronger than the previous one.

5b. *Look at the nail, but don't "aim." Just swing.* Don't argue, just try it.

6. *Practice* (or else you'll "practice" on your first project). Take an old board (like a two-by-four), and as in Steps 1–4, set up a dozen or so nails on the board. Then one by one, drive the nails in as in 5a and 5b. You'll be very pleased that you did this. Trust me. (For commonly used nails, with some tips for how to work with them, see the next chapter, "Nails, Screws, Nuts, and Bolts.")

Once you know how to hammer, you can drive a nail into the average piece of wood, without whacking fiendishly, in about three strokes. And something else happens. In this domain, you become an *older being*, and you will quite naturally pass this ancient wisdom on. Who would have thought that learning how to hammer would make you an historical personage?

SPLITTING

Wood usually splits lengthwise most often when you're nailing near the end of a piece. To avoid splitting:

1. Do not align two adjacent nails on the same line of the grain.

2. When nailing into the actual end of a board (i.e., the part that is cut), first blunt the point. Hold the nail upside-down on a hard surface and tap on it straight down with your hammer.

3. When nailing into hardwood first drill a pilot hole that's slightly smaller than the nail.

TOENAILING

To nail a board perpendicular to another board that is lying flat when you don't have access underneath, you can "toe-nail" by nailing two nails on opposite sides through the upright piece diagonally down into the bottom piece.

Optional Query

There are no instructions on the sides of hammers. *Why aren't there?* (Another million-dollar idea that someone else is going to profit from.)

Nails, Screws, Nuts, and
◆ Bolts—(Very Basic) ◆
Types and Sizes

Civilization is totally fastened together with tiny little nails and screws. So don't be surprised when it turns out that the universe in general is connected together with various kinds of universal fasteners, made of something we probably don't see even if they're right in front of us.

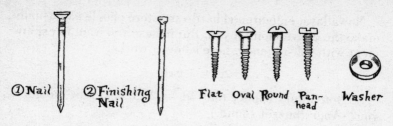

① Nail ② Finishing Nail   Flat Oval Round Pan-head   Washer

Nails

Welcome to the crazy world of nails. There are two common ones you need to know:

1. Nails, which have *flat heads* and look just like, well, nails.

2. Finishing Nails, which have almost no head—only a little bulge for the hammer. Finishing nails are used when you want to protect the wood from hammer blows and to conceal nails inside the wood (like in a cabinet). For this you can use a simple but ambiguously named device called a "nail set" for driving in a finishing nail, cleanly, without banging up the wood.

There are dozens of special nails, but just knowing these two can take you a long way.

Nail Sizes

Even though nails are one of the most important items on Earth, every conceivable effort has been made not to designate the size of nails by any convenient measure, such as inches. Instead, one uses a nail's "penny" size. Furthermore, the symbol for "penny" is *d*, which of course stands for *denarius* (which rhymes with hippocanarius, which is a cross between a hippopotamus and a canary). Look, this isn't my fault. I'm just reporting the news.

Nowadays, enlightened hardware-store people can usually make the conversion for you. But in case you want to experiment with self-reliance, here's how it works:

$$2d = 1 \text{ inch.}$$

So you would expect that 4d = 2 inches, now wouldn't you? (Angry buzzer sound.)

$$6d = 2 \text{ inches.}$$

Just when you think it's all meaningless, a pattern appears. After the first 2d, every 4d adds another inch. (Splitting headache.) So we have . . .

2d = 1, (4d = 1 1/2,) 6d = 2 , 10d = 3, etc.

Ah, but that little "etc." That contains more suffering than a hundred million return trips to the nail store. Because in denarius world 4 inches is not 14d, like it would be in regular nail-world. No, it's *20d*. By now, of course, you've got the idea and have jumped to the illogical conclusion that 5″ is 40d and 6″ is 60d. (How did you know that? Are you a denarian? Say, what do you think? 10,000d! A 7″ nail?)

How big should nails be? In general, approximately two-thirds of the nail's length should be buried in the second or bottom piece (deeper than you might have thought).

Screws (Stronger than Nails and Easier to Remove)

If ever there was a mysterious invention, it was the screw. (Archimedes thought so.) For all I know—and for all you know, unless you're Stephen Hawking or somebody—*black holes* could be formerly used *galactic screw holes*.

Screws usually have a cross slot for a regular screwdriver, or a double-cross slot for a Phillips screwdriver (whose working end mates with the slot).

Common types of screw heads:

Flathead screws are used when the screw is flushed with the surface, or a little below.

Oval-head screws are nicer looking than flatheads and easier to remove. Part of the head is recessed beneath the surface using a drill and a countersink (a tool expressly for this purpose that fits in the drill).

Roundhead screws accept *washers* because the bottom surface of the head is flat. Roundheads are used when the screw must rest above the surface—e.g., if it screws into a very thin piece.

Washers look like Life Savers. These are other tiny little objects without which everything all around us comes apart, or stops working. Washers spread the load of the screw, help make it tight, and protect surfaces from screw marks.

Screw Sizes

Like nails, about one-half to two-thirds of a screw's shank should be embedded in the bottom piece.

The sizing for screws is sensible—lengths are in inches; diameter (the widest part of their shanks) by "gauges." The smaller the gauge, the smaller the diameter. They go from 0 (about $1/16''$) to 24 gauge (about $3/8''$). We won't mention the fact that gauges that apply to the diameter of *wires* go in *reverse*—the lower the gauge, the thicker the wire. (Weird.)

You will definitely run across *sheet-metal* screws for metal-to-metal fastening, most likely, *pan-head screws*—

these are often found on your audio equipment. They are stubby looking, and their heads have distinctive roundish "caps."

─────────── *Nuts & Bolts* ───────────

Bolts have much finer threads than wood screws and shanks that don't taper. Also please remember that nuts screw onto bolts, and we have to stop somewhere, and this is it.

═══════════════════════════════════════

◆ How to Water Houseplants ◆

═══════════════════════════════════════

"Rain don't mean nuthin' to houseplants."
Anonymous

Every genuine organic pursuit possesses *an aura of imprecision,* baffling to many beginners. How can I tell when the food I cook is done? How do I know when to water my plants. And so on. This chapter is dedicated to these newcomers— though other people are allowed to read it.

Our conception of precision is generally rather one-sided. A computer chip, for example, deals with time spans of "nano" seconds and "pico" seconds—a billionth and a *trillionth* of a second, respectively.* Now, this is precision. But knowing just how precise we *need* to be is also an important kind of precision, a precision of appropriateness, a "fuzzy

───────────────────────────────────────

* In spite of the current set of Laws of Physics (these get changed every so often, even though almost no one in any historical period believes *their* set will ever have to be changed), perhaps one day we will achieve the "tax-cut" second, a time span so short that it's over before it begins.

precision." Even though it's as true as bread, this kind of precision to some people seems logically nuts. But suppose you are measuring a space for your potted plant. If you worry about measurements more precise than the nearest inch, it would pinpoint you as somewhat strange—perhaps someone to be observed carefully.

Houseplants provide a perfect environment for developing a feel for the fuzzily precise. Most skilled workers, at least in their specialized area, develop this capacity.

How to Do It

Over-watering is your biggest enemy. "To be safe," many people over-water their plants. This is usually more disastrous than under-watering. If a plant is sick, do not over-water it.

1. Give plants enough water, but don't spoil them. They will have to struggle, but it's an exercise they appreciate and can manage, and it makes them vigorous and happy.

2. When you do water, give plants a real drink. Do not give them only a dribble or two of water. Water thoroughly.

If the plant has been neglected and is very dry, water enough so that it begins to drain out of the bottom. (Throw away the excess water that collects in the saucer or bowl.)

If the soil (and plant) has dried out, you have to soak the whole thing, but for *no more* than an hour. Drain off all excess. A plant should never stand very long in water.

The Finger in the Pot

Here is a guiding rule that plant people know:

3. Put your finger down about an inch into the soil. If the soil is *wet*, do not water; if the soil is *dry*, water immediately and thoroughly.

For most plants, the principal guideline for watering is to water a plant when it is somewhat dry, but not *too* dry. If the soil is fairly *moist*, let it be.

—— *Your Plant and Your Conditions* ——

The knowledge that a particular plant grows in a desert and has thick roots suggests that you will not need to water it very often, but when you do, you should probably water it a lot. Or if a plant grows in the woods, where it's usually humid, or around water, it would most likely possess a finer root structure to soak up moisture in the soil. So you would probably keep this plant more or less continually moist.

You can fine-tune all this by developing that sense of the "fuzzily precise," which arises just from the daily relationship to your living plants, from *looking* at them (and talking to them if no one is around). Plant people know this.

You should understand your particular plants, but you can't get all the practical details from a chart, helpful though it may be, because there are personal variables.

1. A large plant in a small pot requires more water than a small plant in a large pot.

2. Plants in high humidity need less water.

3. Plants near one another require less water because they create their own more humid atmosphere. (Plants are living beings and tend to *like* one another.)

4. The amount of light and the temperature will affect your plant's water requirements. Maybe even the noise has an effect—who knows?

Keep your finger in the pot.

♦ **How to Introduce People** ♦

Introductions are a necessary part of living together in a society, but many of us can't remember our own customs. This produces noticeable anxiety as we waver between wishing to do something the correct way and saying, "The hell with it."

How to Do It

The general rule, like other sensible customs, reinforces a natural inclination:

To the person accorded the most respect, present the other.* You can simply say the name of the most respected party first.

"Zeus, this is Bob." More formally, "Zeus, I'd like to present Ulysses." With this rule alone you can manage.

To be at ease with the traditional courtesies means just to recognize a few basic situations where people have generally agreed to apply a particular hierarchy of respect:

1. **Rank is first, regardless of sex;**
2. **women next, then**
3. **by age.**
4. **The host and hostess always rise and *shake hands* with their guests regardless of all other conventions.**

1. **Rank. The most respected, above all, are pro-**

---

* The main reason why almost everyone is so confused is that when writers describe the order of introduction, the *first* name they mention in the sentence *is the person whose name is pronounced last!*

spective employers. (Especially in troubled times.) Then, superiors in a business firm, heads of Church or State, tribal chiefs, or anybody very distinguished or very elderly.

"Ulysses, this is Chip Dudley, fullback for Troy State."

If none of the above applies:

2. To a woman, a man is presented.

"Circe, this is Ulysses." And optionally you may add, "Ulysses, Circe."*

3. Age. To adults, children are presented, and usually the relationship is included.

"Apollo, this is my son, Icarus."

4. Do not say, "This is Mr. Claus" if you are Mrs. Claus. Say, "This is my husband." Or, "This is my husband, Santa."

Some Details

Instead of overwhelming you with numerous gettings-up and not-gettings-up, let's just say that:

1. A woman does not rise for a man unless she is the host or unless his "rank" takes precedence.

2. Even older men (except the very elderly) traditionally rise for a grown woman, young or old.

3. Men shake hands with one another, but a man shakes hands with a woman only if the woman offers first. But if a man is excited and extends his hand, you would be a clod to refuse. Europeans shake hands much more than Americans do.

4. Topics. Unless you are moved to say something relevant, when introduced just say normal twentieth-century things (unless it's the twenty-first century) like "Hello" or

---

* Medusa would be an exception. There are always exceptions to any procedure, and you have to use common sense. So in this case an appropriate introduction might be: "Ulysses, don't look now, but Medusa has her eyes on you."

"How do you do?" or "Nice to meet you" (even if it isn't). Other-century, and noncentury expressions like "Charmed, I'm sure" are ridiculous.

It is customary—especially if you are the host or hostess —to add some words to help get the conversation started, often about the weather.

"Zeus, this is Ulysses. He's curious about tomorrow's weather."

Or merchandising: "Achilles, this is Stosh Jamison. He says he has some wood for that horse." Or some other mutually engaging topic:

"Penelope, this is Ulysses, your long-lost husband."

What if . . .

. . . You can't remember the name of someone you met once last year at a dinner? Just relax and say something like "I'm sorry, I've forgotten your name."

But what if it's someone with whom you've recently had a lengthy, high-spirited exchange? What if it's your best friend? (You can think of other embarrassing realities.)

In these circumstances, *do not tell the truth* and say, *"I've forgotten your name."* (Egad!)

Just look at the person whose name you *don't* know and, using the name of the person you *do* know, say, "I'd like you to meet Helen."

Then smile at both of them and leave quickly to take care of something important.* This method also has the advantage of stimulating a lively exchange between the newly acquainted:

"Helen, it's nice to meet you."

---

* If you don't remember either name, you can leave even more quickly with an even bigger smile.

"It's nice to meet you. But I didn't get your—"

"Paris."

"Paris. A memorable name."

"How about we explore upstairs?"

◆ How to Iron a Shirt ◆

For unknown and possibly deep reasons, there are certain procedures that create *mad adherents*. These are people who swear dogmatically to the point of dueling that their particular method is the only correct method and should be adopted right away by everybody. The force with which they declare their position is always out of proportion to the task at hand. This is particularly noticeable when two mad adherents meet. Both of them rave like lunatics over the stupidity of the other's perfectly good method (rational behavior, I guess, if one is mad).

Some procedures that particularly attract this behavior are poaching eggs (not included in this book for fear of reprisals), sharpening knives, and *ironing shirts*. I don't know why these. This is just a news report.

How to Do It

Ironing is essentially quiet—even when *sshhwooossshh* goes the steam.

1. Heat up the iron to the "cotton" or "polyester" setting, or whatever setting represents your shirt.

2. Dampen the shirt slightly. Ideally it's already

damp from the dryer, which makes everything go splendidly. If not, it has been well-known for centuries, perhaps millennia, that if you spray or, better yet, *flick* water on a shirt (there seems to be a verb for almost everything), roll it up carefully, and let it stand for half an hour, then ironing will once again go splendidly. In such cases, turn off the steam.

3. To avoid burning the shirt, don't deploy the iron on one spot for more than a few seconds at a time. You have to be a little more careful about burning the shirt when you iron a damp spot. But if you meet a stubborn wrinkle, *spray* water on it and try again. Dribbling, trickling, or flicking water onto the shirt while ironing is inefficient and silly. Some irons have a spray feature, but even better is to use one of those little plastic spray bottles for houseplants. This makes ironing smooth going.

THE ORDER OF IRONING (some adherents will froth at the mouth)

Consider the four parts of a shirt:

Yoke (i.e., the shoulders and the in-between part just under the collar)
Collar
Sleeves
Back & Sides, which ultimately become the Fronts

The order of ironing is very important. The idea is not to wrinkle some already-completed portion. There are *many* possible ironing orders (one of the items that mad adherents pontificate about). The order given here works; if you have a better one, I am very happy for you.

1. Iron the yoke. Incidentally, the yoke of a shirt is an outstanding manifestation of *The Law of Saucers* (pg. 37) because when you think of a shirt, you do not immediately think of the intermediate zone that is the yoke (unless you are the person in the factory responsible for producing yokes).

The collar is a very noticeable part, but usually not as prone to wrinkle as the sides or the sleeves.

2a. Iron the collar on the _reverse_ side (do this first).

2b. Iron the collar on the front side, lightly and gently, from the tips in toward the center. This is opposite to the way you might think.

3a. Iron the sleeves—doing both sides of each sleeve.

3b. Iron the _inside_ and the outside of each cuff.

4. Finish by ironing a side, then the back, then the remaining side. The tip of the iron will help you maneuver carefully around the buttons.

Which reminds me. Ironing is a great job for practicing . . .

The Law of Craft: Try to do something well without thinking about sex or dinner.

——— *Optional—Winter Ironing* ———

If you always wear sweaters in winter—and you are especially short on time (and you hate ironing)—you may wish to consider the extremely dubious, hypocritical, and scandalous procedure which is called "winter ironing." Winter ironing is when you iron only those parts of the shirt that show while wearing a sweater; i.e., the collar, the throat, and the yoke—forget the cuffs.

This is shocking.

How to Remember
Jokes and Stories

One of life's mysteries: People who remember baseball line-ups for all the major-league teams for the past thirty-five years can't recall a simple joke to tell at dinner. This is one of the very deep strangenesses of human consciousness. On the surface it can be "explained" by . . .

The Law of Seriousness: If everyone remembered jokes, life would consist mostly of trading jokes.

To prevent this, joke-remembering is distributed to a select, random group. The rest of us are generally doomed to be joke morons. Is there anything we can do to climb out of this lowly estate?

The *Law of Constellations* (pg. 47) reveals that the most important physical entities in the universe (the stars) are generally unremembered or ignored, except by specialists. Jokes seem to be in the same category. (Maybe jokes and stories are among the most important items on Earth. Just kidding.)

But the remedy is the same. You have to approach this as if you actually wanted someone to learn something. You study, you reinforce, you learn some more, you review, etc. Like *learning something*. Please don't forget that one of the great boons of learning is that the more familiar you become with a subject, the more interesting it usually gets.

You are someone who can remember the intricate sequence of getting dressed, complicated cookie recipes, or byzantine movie plots, and therefore you can certainly remember jokes —especially if they happened to you.

1. When you're trying to remember a joke for future recall, put yourself in the picture (which can be quite funny in itself).

2. Write the main points down in sketchy note form. Pay special regard to the *punch-line*. Any slip-ups, retractions, or (unintentional) hesitations in the final moments of drama, will drastically reduce, or completely nullify the story's impact.

3. Tell the joke to someone new every day for five days. At the end of five days, look at what you wrote. It's a straightforward learning method. Sure if you were one of the "joke-select," you wouldn't have to learn it this way. It would just come through your pores.

But undoubtedly you are a "something"-select—with respect to some activity that you really didn't have to learn the way the rest of us had to. It could be cooking, baseball, dancing, sewing, car repair, music, fashion trending, or making friends. Whatever it is, it just seems easy. You may not even realize how good you are at whatever it is because it comes so naturally.

Theme and Variation—How to ___
Overcome the Fear of Invention

If you are afflicted with the extremely common Fear of Invention, it is partly (or wholly) because you don't believe that you have a right to change the universe in any way outside of your allotted activities.

4. It's okay to vary the joke. (It's still the same joke.) Change the characters, change the locale, change the details. (It's the same joke.) Perhaps change even the penguins, if it has penguins (or perhaps not). In any case, suddenly you will realize that the joke is no longer quite the same. *You have changed the joke*. A slightly new joke. You have made your own personal waves.

NOTE: All "waves" can be ultimately broken down into electromagnetic waves, and it is known that these waves—for instance, all of the "Ozzie and Harriet" radio programs from the 1940s—proceed outward from the Earth into SPACE *at the speed of light*, spreading FOREVER throughout the ENTIRE COSMOS. Imagine—Ozzie and Harriet, wowing them in the Andromeda Galaxy!

◆ The Essential Down-to-Earth ◆
Kitchen Measurements

This may sound strange, but you can cook really well—*even bake*, in spite of what they tell you—without knowing how to measure anything officially (i.e., with measuring cups and

103

spoons). Yet it definitely helps to know a few basic measurements.

> **2 sticks butter = ½ lb. = 1 cup**
> **(1 stick butter = ¼ lb. = ½ cup)**
> **5 large eggs = 1 cup (approx.)**
> **⅞ cup unsifted flour = 1 cup sifted flour**

The need for sifting flour is overrated. For a fine cake, probably. For most breads and any quick bread, it is utterly unnecessary. Just remember that it takes a little less unsifted flour to equal a cup than sifted, since unsifted flour is more densely packed. Once you see how much less (about ⅛ of a cup), you will easily be able to "eyeball" the right amount of unsifted flour.

NOTE: If the weather is muggy, humid, or wet, any measured quantity of flour will contain somewhat more flour than you want. Why? Because the flour is more densely packed. So cut back a little. Of course, you can *weigh* the flour. But if you're already doing that, then you already know everything in this chapter.

The Liquid Basics

> **3 teaspoons (3t) = 1 Tablespoon (T)**
> **2 Tablespoons = 1 oz. (= 1 coffee-cup measure)**
> **4 Tablespoons (4T) = ¼ cup**
> **1 Cup = 8 oz.**
> **1 Quart = 32 oz.**

How to Fly a Kite—An Introduction

◆

How to Launch (and Land) a Kite

A "kite" is a system. It includes the kite, the string, and you. Find an open space with *no power lines*. If large trees are swaying dramatically, *leave your kite at home*. ◄ If a storm is coming up, kite flying can actually be dangerous. ►

LAUNCHING

People are no longer being encouraged to launch a kite running into the wind. Progress has deemed it more becoming to stand still—even if it means going to great lengths, involving an accomplice, and so on. Though children and grown-ups have been executing running launches for thousands of years, these moderns say that you might stumble or trip. (Playing tag may be fingered next.)

Okay, so I did try launching a kite without running, and I admit it was good! You need a bit of a breeze to do it alone.

1. Hold the kite up with your back to the wind, and when a gust comes along, just toss it up into the wind. Very satisfying.

2. As the kite ascends, steadily pay out the line—but not so fast that you lose tension, or the kite will lose power.

3. The stronger the wind, the faster you can pay

out the line. (Sometimes moving backward quickly will keep the line taut.) If you don't let the line out fast enough, there will be too much tension, the kite will climb too fast for the short line, and it may loop over into a dive.

4. If your kite is going crazy while still at a low altitude (higher up, a "dancing" kite is a desired thrill), **just slacken the line completely; when the kite calms down, pull the line in to send it back up.**

5. Tugging on the line increases the angle the kite makes with the wind, which causes it to rise (which is good). Sometimes it's a real pull, sometimes just a twitch.

6. If the kite is not exerting a pull upward (i.e., ascending), then letting out line tends to flatten the angle and move it off toward the horizon (also good). Your kite thrives when you skillfully execute both actions— mastered by trying. Once the kite is aloft, alternate giving short tugs (and occasionally longer pulls) with letting out line. These are your primary piloting activities. No matter how high up or far away, the kite "feels" everything you do.

7. Tails, etc. If the kite twitches and darts, add more tail; if the kite has difficulty rising and the tail isn't streaming in the wind, then shorten it. (Eventually you will be manipulating tails, "bridles," and "towing rings," depending on the weather.)

8. Landing—reel in gradually, while moving toward the kite. At the very end, slacken the line.

THE RUNNING LAUNCH

Why not experience launching a kite the "real" way (i.e., "stumbling and falling")? **Just look at the path in front of you (be sure it's clear), set the kite on the ground, and run into the wind, paying out the line as before.** Think of all those old drawings of girls and boys running with their kites. You can't just throw all that away. You might as will kiss the lions good-bye—or chocolate.

Why Do Kites Fly?

A kite's shape, structure, and rigging causes it to lean into the wind at an upward angle. Blowing across the bottom, the wind acts like a wedge, forcing the kite upward and back. Since the string keeps the kite from proceeding too far back, the only way the kite can move—if it is light enough—is up.

An additional factor is the Bernoulli Principle, demonstrable by anyone who can blow out a candle, yet it was supposedly not known in relation to kites until the nineteenth century.*

How Come Nobody Noticed It Before?

It's 1728 and my friend Daniel and I are sitting in a tavern somewhere in the Italian Swiss Alps. On the table is a scrap of (eighteenth-century) paper.

What do you think, Bob? If I blow down on this paper, will it rise up?

"No, why should it?"

Good question. Would you like to see a demonstration?

"You're going to make that piece of paper fly up by blowing down on it. You're losing it, Dan."

Watch.

(He blows down on the paper at a slight angle, putting his hand behind it so it won't blow off the table. The scrap of

---

* The world had to wait until Sir George Cayley, the inventor of the glider, demonstrated the Bernoulli Principle's application to gliding—by (would you believe?) blowing a piece of paper across a table.

paper clearly rises up as it moves forward. Now, you would think that an average bloke like me would have to get pretty excited, right?)

"So, okay, it rose up. Big deal."

Bob, you don't get it. It rose up.

"Yeah, well, you *blew* on it. Of course it rose up. Anyone can do that. Anyone can blow on a piece of paper."

But airplanes—!

"Airplanes?"

I got carried away. Birds, then. KITES!

"Dave, I like you anyway. You're a little strange, but hey, that's okay. I'll bet you've been working on those equators again."

Equations. Do you know how a kite flies?

"We need some cappuccino here. We left Basel for ski country and now we're blowing on scraps of paper."

Well? (Daniel looks serious.)

"The wind blows the kite up in the air. When the wind stops, the kite falls down."

That's true, actually. But I'm not sure you understand—

"Chocolate or cinnamon?"

Cinnamon?

Daniel never talked to anyone else about his kite theories, but he became a beloved and famous scientist anyway, which shows you what a serious, wondering person without expensive equipment can do.* (However, no one in the eighteenth century has ever heard of *me*. They can't even find my records.)

——— *The Bernoulli Principle* ———

Daniel came up with his principle that the faster a

---

* Daniel Bernoulli is considered the first mathematical physicist.

fluid moves, the less pressure it exerts on whatever is around it.* This makes sense; e.g., if water is traveling rapidly, say through a tube, most of the molecules don't have time to get distracted bumping into walls. They're on the move.

So, if air goes faster *above* a kite (or an airplane wing) than it does *below*, there will be more pressure exerted from below, which becomes "lift."†

◆ How to Sharpen a Knife ◆

A knife is a kind of chisel. From the chisel comes the file, and from the file, in one form or another, come all of our tools—or the tools that make the rest of our tools. Therefore, the chisel may be the source of all of our technology. The hammer people disagree, but that's show business.

Basically, there are two kinds of knives that most of us ever have to sharpen: a *carving knife* (which is sharpened on a piece of "steel") and a *pocket knife* (usually sharpened on a small oilstone, or "whetstone").

The key unit of knowledge for sharpening these knives is the number **15** (as in *15 degrees*). This is the distance away from the steel or, stone that you tilt a knife when sharpening. (Don't get tense. You just do it approximately.)

If you simply know this number—15—you can sharpen! And the great thing about 15 is that nothing else is 15 anything; e.g., there aren't 15 players on a team or 15

* Water and air are both fluids.
† Of course, there were kite-fliers three thousand years before Daniel, but they were just lucky.

ounces in a pound. (There are fifteen object balls in pocket billiards, but they're *round*.)

— *How to Do It—The Carving Knife* —

1. **Hold the knife in your favored hand and the steel in the other.**
2. **Set the heel of the blade, with its face toward you, at a 15° angle against the top of the steel.**
3. **Stroke downward while pulling the handle toward you, making sure that the entire length of the blade makes contact with the steel.**
4. **For the next stroke, start with the blade on the opposite side of the steel.**
5. **Repeat both strokes three or four times.**
The folklore is to . . .
6. **Pretend that you are *slicing off a piece of the steel*, using light to medium pressure.** The sense of the blade hugging the steel as it moves is very satisfying.
7. **Once in a long while, depending on use, have all of your good knives sharpened by a professional.** (Often your butcher can have it done for you.)
8. **Wash and dry your valuable knives separately.** Put them away immediately in the knife block, knife rack, or knife drawer (where they should not be in contact with one another). Remember that other utensils get a perverse pleasure out of banging up costly knives when everything's thrown together in a sink.

— *How to Do It—The Pocket Knife* —

Use a small, lightly oiled stone—or (if no one is watching) you can spit on the stone. The idea is that the oil or spit acts like a slurry that fills in the minute irregular pits on the stone so that the knife will sharpen evenly.

1. It's essentially the same procedure as for the carving knife, but simpler. With a pocket knife, the entire blade may fit easily on the stone without having to make any extra side motions.

2. After a few strokes, feel the edge of the blade by running your fingers down the flat portion.

3. There should be a "feather edge" on both sides, which means you're almost done.

4. Run the knife lightly on each side to remove this edge. When you look at the blade in the light, ideally there should be no *shiny spots*—which, oddly enough, are portions of the blade that are *dull* (another life surprise).

Knots You Need, and Knots You Don't

Almost every kid between the ages of eight and fourteen once spent forty minutes with a knot book. It takes that long to figure out the drawings, or to figure out that you can't figure out the drawings since usually the knots are shown *already tightened.* But you feel a trace of guilt for not learning all those knots the knot writers told you were so important.

The Square Knot is unquestionably an all-galactic construction. Without Square Knots, a large portion of civilized reality would speedily come undone. (Your *shoes* certainly would. See "How to Tie Your Shoes," pg. 188.) With this knot alone you can tie up almost anything. Square Knots lie flat, making them excellent for tying bandages, bundles, or two similar ropes together—you name it.

But how many knots do you really need to know how to tie? A Square Knot, maybe a couple of "hitches," possibly a Packer's Knot for securing packages and loads—and that's it. Of course, sailors, cowboys, mathematicians, and hangmen need to fathom various other knots, but chances are *you* don't.

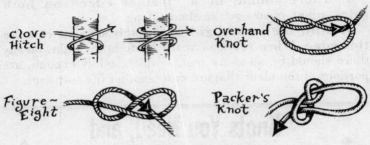

Knots You Need

I have added a few ideas here and there to help you remember these knots better. Some of these tips you won't find in knot books. Why? Because the authors are so good at knots they don't realize how hard it is for many of us to learn them. You think I'm exaggerating? Pick up one of these lengthy Ph.D. knot treatises for yourself.

Every knot you need is a simple translation or extension of the *Overhand Knot*, the first knot everybody learns.

The Overhand Knot Comes First

Visualize an **Overhand Knot** as wrapping a rope one-half turn around itself and then through the loop formed. There are two kinds of Overhands: You can start with the right side in front of the left, i.e., *right-over-left*. Or the opposite, *left-over-right*.

The **Square Knot** consists of two Overhand knots, but the second Overhand is tied *opposite* to the first—no matter which Overhand you begin with. The Square Knot may be tied using the two ends of the same rope, or the ends of two different ropes.

If you should mistakenly use the *same* Overhand both times, such as right-over-left, then right-over-left again, you will tie the DREADED **Granny Knot.** This is a horrid knot because not only does a Granny wait to come undone at the most critical and embarrassing times—possibly ruining your life—but paradoxically, it's harder to untie on purpose than a Square Knot! A good knot should be strong but fairly easy to untie.

If you want a bigger knot that is even more secure against accidental undoing, then add another Overhand Knot, or even another Square Knot, to the first.

Hitches

Use a hitch when you want to attach a rope to a (hitching) post, a ring, or a mooring. Hitches can be made very rapidly, and the harder you pull on the rope, the tighter the rope binds to the object (like a noose). The **Clove Hitch** and the **Half-Hitch** are both simple variants of the Overhand Knot.

The **Clove Hitch** is a rope wrapped twice around something.

1. Start wrapping the rope up the pole in a spiral —with the working end crossing **over** the first layer of rope.

2. Start the second wrap—put the working end **under** the diagonal rope as in the figure. *That's the key.* As the second wrap comes around, simply tuck it under itself.

The ends should be going in opposite directions and it should look handsome.

If you can cast a loop over an object—like a post—then you can make a Clove Hitch like a real sailor.

1a. Form two *identical* loops by placing the right side of the rope over the left for both loops. (Don't reverse this even if you're left-handed).

2a. Put the second loop formed *under* the first—that's the "key"—and slip the whole business over the post. Pull on the two ends, which should always be going in opposite directions. The second time you try this it takes less than four seconds.

You can make the Clove Hitch more secure by adding *Two Half-Hitches* ($\frac{1}{2} + \frac{1}{2} = 1$).

A **Half-Hitch** is an Overhand Knot with one simple difference: The working end of the rope is pulled in the opposite direction from the way you would pull it to form a regular Overhand Knot. It's as though you don't quite finish the Overhand before you pull the end tight. This may help you remember how to tie Half-Hitches even if you don't tie one for five years.

And, of course, there are Timber Hitches, Witches Hitches, even a Hitch named Ralph, but you don't need any of them.

The Packer's Knot

Packages, as well as loads on a pickup or on the roof of your car, are best secured with rope tightened with a **Packer's Knot,** which once learned also takes about three seconds to tie. I do, of course, recognize that having to secure thousands of loads throughout your life in all kinds of nutty circumstances, you have probably developed some kind of (probably nutty) method that also works.

From childhood, remember the **Figure-Eight?** If you think of an Overhand knot as wrapping around itself *one-half turn before* you put the end through the loop that is formed, then a Figure-Eight simply wraps around itself a *full turn before* going through the loop formed. Pull to tighten. (Really easy.)

To make the **Packer's Knot:**

1. Wrap the working end of the rope around the STANDING PART (the nonworking end) one full turn.

2. Then make a Figure-Eight with the working end and one side of the loop you've just made—as if the rest of it weren't there. The result is a strong Slip Knot* with a Figure-Eight at the "throat." To tighten, grasp the large loop and pull away from the Figure-Eight part.

3. The two ends of the rope must be going in the same direction. If they aren't, then **reverse the initial wrap around the standing part.** (You can also view this knot as just a Figure-Eight around the STANDING PART.)

The First Law of Knots: The STANDING PART doesn't do anything, but neither does zero, mountaintops, or the centers of wheels.

——— *Knots Can Drive You Nuts* ———

One knot, intensively touted in knot books is the Bowline (pronounced *"bow*-l'n"). The main purpose of this knot is to create a large nonslipping loop. This may be an essential

---

* A knot that slips along a rope, enlarging and shrinking its loop as it moves. (A noose is a kind of Slip Knot.)

knot for sailors and other specific professionals (like helicopter rescuers), but it is shown here to emphasize what insidious salespeople most knot writers are. They always tell you how useful, how thrilling, and how obligatory it is for you to know how to tie a Bowline. Of course, *you will never tie a Bowline again.*

However, it was never my intention to reject useless knowledge that's interesting for it's own sake. One way to remember this knot so that you can demonstrate it as a knot most of us don't need to know:

The rabbit goes up the hole, gets understanding, then goes back down.* This means you start by making an Overhead Loop in the STANDING PART (the part that's not doing anything), then put the working end *up through the loop*, then *under the standing part*, and finally *down through the original loop.*

Long may the Bowline live—even for landlubbers!

◆ How to Replace a Lamp Plug ◆ (and Other Simple Plugs)

You told me this book wasn't going to include anything really hard, let alone impossible. But not only does changing a plug have to do with *mechanical facility* (opening up something mysterious), it also involves *electricity.*

So what.

How can you just sit there, smug like that?

* A variation on knot-lore.

No, no, listen. This is almost as easy as making toast. *Electricity* has *nothing* to do with changing a lamp plug. Why? *Because nothing is plugged in until after you're done.* I am ready to attack a plug.

— *How to Do It—Basic Plug Method* —

Basic Plugs accept cords that aren't too thick, which is your average lamp plug and most other plugs. One way to tell that what you have is a Basic Plug is that it's *plug-shaped.*

There are other plugs that aren't plug-shaped—e.g., they might be cone-shaped or funnel-shaped. These often accept thicker cords, so you have to use the Advanced Plug Method, described below.

There are two possible kinds of Basic Plugs.

BASIC PLUG #1 IS A SINGLE UNIT WITH ONE MOVABLE PART

1. Cut the cord straight across a little below the plug with cutters or a knife.

2. Get an electric, or "lamp," plug that lets you *snap* **or** *squeeze* **the cord in without having to strip it.** (It's okay to ask a salesperson to get one for you.)

3. Insert the cord into the small opening, usually on the side of the plug. This cord always consists of *two wires,* but is insulated by covers and melded together. You do not have to separate these wires. You do not have to "strip" these wires. *In fact, you don't have to do anything except insert the cord into the slot.*

4. Press down on the plug's movable part to finish the job. This part has two sharp metal "points" that dig through the cord's insulation and make contact with the wires within.

BASIC PLUG #2 HAS AN INNER PIECE AND AN OUTER PIECE
The outer piece is a "shell" and looks just like a regular "plug." Everything is just as easy:

1. Insert the cord up through the small opening in the outer piece and the inner piece. The cord deadends inside the inner piece. Okay so far.

2. Shove the inner piece into the outer piece. And everything good will happen automatically.

Now it's true that I'm not really telling you anything that the directions on a Basic Plug don't already tell you, but at least you know that Basic Plugs exist!

How to Do It—The Advanced Plug Method

HOW TO STRIP A WIRE AND ATTACH IT TO A TERMINAL
For larger plugs that accept thicker cords, often round or funnel-shaped, you do have to actually (oh, no) "strip" a wire, and (I'm fainting) loosen two screws, tie a simple knot (tell me it's lies), wrap the wires around the shanks of the screws, and (help, police or somebody) tighten the screws.

A simple tool called a **Wire-Stripper** does the job in two minutes and twelve seconds—two minutes to locate the tool, four seconds to separate the insulation between the two wires, *and four seconds to strip each of the two wires.*

1. Separate by hand the pair of wires that make up the cord—for at least an inch.

2. Insert one of the wires into whatever *hole* in the wire-stripper it fits easily and snugly. If you know the "gauge" (diameter) of the wire, it's listed by each hole.

Holding the wire in one hand and the stripper perpendicular to the wire in the other hand . . .

3. Pull the tool across about one-half inch of the wire—and off. The tool strips away the insulation.

4. Repeat for the neighboring wire. (You can do all this with a knife but be careful not to cut the wire itself.)

HOW TO ATTACH THE WIRES
Remove the cardboard cover over the inside of the plug.

5. Push the two wires up through the hole in the end of the plastic cover and tie them into a simple Overhand Knot. (This is the kind you start with when you *tie your shoes.*) Pull this knot tight between the two socket prongs. The purpose of this knot is to help your new plug survive a couple of decades of careless yanking out of sockets by someone pulling on the wire instead of the plug.

A nifty knot that has been invented for this occasion—the Underwriter's Knot—allows the plug to survive a couple of decades plus one extra. (You can look this up in some other book.)

6. Curl one of the bare wires clockwise almost all the way around the terminal (under the screwhead) and screw it down.

7. Do likewise with the other bare wire on the other terminal, curling it clockwise.

To achieve 5, 6, and 7 you may have to poke, pull, or fuss around a little. This is educational and good.

CAUTION: Never allow part of a bare wire to touch a neighboring wire. This creates a "short circuit," which isn't good for your lamp. It is also likely to blow a fuse (see "How to Change a Fuse," pg. 79).

Put back the cardboard cover, if any. If necessary, bend slightly to fit.

Optional

A common, worrisome question that people sometimes have about wires and terminals arises when the terminals are different colors, usually BRASS and SILVER—and the wires are also different colors, usually BLACK and WHITE. Which wire goes to which terminal?

In such cases, hook the WHITE wire to the SILVER terminal (makes sense). This is also what everyone does anyway when they don't know and don't remember.

◆ How to Repair a Lamp ◆

Jeff: Look, I'm pointing my flashlight up into the sky.
Do you want to walk up the beam?
Mutt: I know that trick. You'll turn it off in the middle.
Early memories of Mutt and Jeff

I must admit that if this book were a textbook (which it isn't), then this chapter would go near the beginning as a model for addressing *The Fear of Taking Things Apart*, also known as The Fear of Adjusting an Object Without Manufacturer's Instructions or (Heaven help you) Looking Inside. Now, I'm certainly not suggesting that you start stripping down your C.D. player, your computer, or your refrigerator motor and fiddle with their insides. But there are some objects that you could look into.

Lamps are one of these objects. In fact, it would be well worthwhile to dig up that old, inoperable lamp made of unknown weird materials—the one your Aunt Boris gave you (if you have an Aunt Boris, it is almost for sure that you received one of these lamps). This is your what-the-hell lamp, and is *your ticket to inanimate-object fearlessness.*

How to Do It

Make sure you don't have a burnt-out light bulb. (After all this, how embarrassing.) *Is it plugged in?* (Even more embarrassing.) Did you plug it in somewhere else to make sure it's not a defective receptacle? (Is the plug damaged? If so, *it's not a lamp problem.* Refer to the previous chapter on "How to Replace a Lamp Plug.")

Lamp repair is a model for the *Great Law of Undoing:*

> **The Great Law of Undoing:** The Original (Defective) Condition + Undoing + Doing = the Original (Fixed) Condition.

Repairing a lamp is the perfect medium in which to find a new level of confidence in relation to this important Law. Why? Because lamp repair sounds horribly complicated, yet once you know how to replace a lamp plug (see previous chapter), it's as easy as taking off your clothes and putting them back on. The most important step is the decision to *get up and do it*.

Please look at Aunt Boris's lamp, or any lamp that is before you. What is it? (This is an excellent question to ask when you're in front of something incomprehensible.) From your present point of view as a lamp repairer, a lamp is merely a bulb screwed into a switch/socket (we'll just call it a "socket") with a pair of wires attached to its terminals, which go to a plug that plugs into the wall. That's a lamp.

What can go wrong with it? The socket or the wires that make up the lamp cord—or both. (We have already discussed the wall plug.) What will you do?

Get a screwdriver, wire strippers (a pocket knife is not as good, but usable), and if necessary a pair of pliers to unscrew things with. Open up the lamp, remove the socket and wires, get new ones at the store, close the lamp back up in reverse, test it, and have a cup of tea or something.

To get started:

1. Remove the bulb and the shade. You might have to unscrew something. If the lamp has a "harp" (harp-shaped metal prongs that hold the shade), remove it, pressing the prongs together—presto! It comes off. Also remove the felt piece, if any, from under the base. If not, look for some more nuts to unscrew.

There are many ways to proceed, now that you know how to replace a lamp plug, because the same wiring procedure holds for the socket.

2. Open up the lamp and note—even write down if need be—the order of the removal of items. If there's anything else not on the above "lamp list" that should mosey out, or fall out of your Aunt Boris's lamp; e.g., if a lead weight the size of an elephant emerges from the base, it's

122

okay. Just put everything back when you're done.

3. Once you know how to attach wires, the whole thing is about as difficult as screwing and un-screwing. The socket itself, for instance, has sleeves that come off.* Remove them. Maybe they will "click" back together later on. You'll find out. It's no big deal.

4. You may have to feed a cord *through a tube*! (Egad!) You may even have to go to the hardware store to get a new socket and cord. Though they're likely to be standard, you can take the old items with you for comfort.†

NOTE: Remember to tie an Overhand Knot in the wires that go into the socket. It is also helpful to tie an Overhand Knot in the cord just before it comes out of the lamp base to reduce strain on the cord when yanked or pulled.

5. Test the lamp (with a bulb in it). Be proud of yourself—even if it doesn't work! The lighting in a lamp is straightforward, so try to find out what isn't right. Aunt Boris would be grateful for a successful conclusion—or, really, any news from the front.

---

* A socket consists of a metal outer shell that contains a cardboard or plastic insulating sleeve that shields it from the inside aluminum shell—the one that the bulb actually screws into. Take the outer shell off by pressing at the base where (this is unbelievable) IT ACTUALLY SAYS "PRESS." I hope the considerate person who revealed this big "PRESS" secret got off better than, say, Prometheus.
† Some lamps with large three-way bulbs have very wide "mogul" sockets (a great word).

◆ How to Learn a Foreign Language ◆ While You're on the Plane

People who learn languages know that the "secret" is obvious: *words*. The grammatical requirements are minimal; e.g., *Tarzan know English*.

I assume you have a dictionary and a book that contains some basic grammar. This chapter can supplement these, and it includes word lists and ultra-minimum grammar.

Pronunciation

Definitely make every effort to learn how to pronounce the language. Most languages are much more consistent in this regard than English, which is insane. Native speakers will appreciate your efforts many times over. Of course, you will, to their ears, sound "foreign." But it will be acceptable, possibly even charming.

Pay attention to the vowel sounds. English does strange things to the vowels of other languages. Our vowel sounds are "impure," as there is usually another vowel mixed in—often at the end—we pronounce "day" as "day-ee." Try not to carry over the full dose of this unintentional sloppiness.

Quick Word List

List One is the basic forty to fifty words. With these alone you can get around. You can even get in and out of many situations (if you want to). Most people can learn these words while flying on an airplane for more than eight hours to another world—especially if you use the AMAZING FLASH CARDS (described at the end of List One).

NOTE: Related words or phrases may be found on the same line, separated by commas. Synonymous words or phrases are also on the same line but separated by slashes (/)—these can usually be translated by the same word.

LIST ONE

pardon me
please, thank you, you're welcome
hello/how are you (the daily greeting)
good evening (good night) (night greetings), good-bye
yes, no
where is
rest room
bank
taxi
train station
airport
right, left, straight ahead
do you have . . . ?
how much
I don't speak [whatever language], I don't understand
slower
I need
help
waiter, the check
I'll come back/return
tomorrow
I can, I can't, can I?, can you?

come, go,

I must, I must [go, or some other verb]

for

and, but

good, bad

all/everything, nothing

happy, tired

charming/nice

very, very much/a lot, too much

fantastic/great/wonderful (the common affirmative exclamation)

here, there

I would like (to have) . . . Would you like . . . ?

change, please

what?/what is it?

I am an [American, or whatever]/I am from [America or wherever]

I, you, he/she/it we, you, they (*subject pronouns*)

to be (conjugate present tense)

to have (conjugate present tense)

me, you (*object pronouns*—if they exist)

not (forming negatives)

? (forming questions)

I through 10 (numbers)

very common idiomatic words (like *gemütlich,* German for genial, cozy, comfortable) and common social expressions.

_____ *How to Use Home-Made, or* _____ *Airplane-Made, Flash Cards*

This method is thousands of years old and has never been improved upon.

1. **Use three-by-five cards cut in half—or tear up some (airplane) stationery.** (Perfect rectangles are not obligatory.) There is *genuine learning magic* when items to memorize are on rearrangeable little pieces of paper (the first word processor!) instead of frozen together on a list.

2. **Write the foreign word on one side and its English equivalent on the other.**

3. **First practice translating from the other language to English.**

4. **Shuffle the cards at every whim**—one of the greatnesses of flash cards.

5. **Practice until you can go through *very quickly*, without stopping to think.**

6. **Then go from English to the other language.**

7. *Keep mixing up those cards.*

You may be pleasantly surprised at how fast you can learn this way. Of course, you also have to practice saying simple sentences OUT LOUD (if you don't have a seatmate)—and out loud to yourself if you do—unless that person is helping you. (Respect their privacy. Do not be rude.)

I hope (after a break—perhaps a movie) you review List One, and then learn List Two (use flash cards). You can then have real conversations!

On Listening

Let the words flow by. If you stop on a word you don't know, you lose the next five. Try to maintain a rhythm of listening.

LIST TWO

How do you say [whatever it is] in [whatever the language]?
What does [word in the other language] mean?

this, that (adj., pro.)
hurry
also
what time is it?/o'clock
when?
who?
with
eat, drink
it's possible/perhaps
why?, because
paper, newspaper, book
now
day (e.g., "I am here three days"), week, month, year
there is, there are (usually different), here is
today
morning, evening
(show agreement) I agree/it's true/of course
big, small
crazy, bored
find, Can you find . . . ?
love, know
remember, forget, think, believe
do, work
thanks anyway

FOOD (water, coffee, tea, milk, cream, lemon, bread, butter, salt, pepper, beer, [liquor], and special needs

some universal words: okay, American

some European Universal words: okay, pardon, ciaou (casual greeting), good-bye, restaurant, hotel

wife, husband, son, daughter, father, mother, sister, brother

About Word Lists

1. You are allowed to learn other words that are not on these lists.

2. Learn opposite or related words at the same time. (A basic learning trick.)

3. Learn the gender when first learning the noun —as if it were part of the word. Most languages divide all nouns (and often the adjectives that modify them) into masculine, feminine, and sometimes even neuter (e.g., German). Except for the obvious "girl," "boy," etc., these ancient assignments often have no apparent relationship to the meaning.

4. Learn how to make plurals.

Ultra-Minimum Grammar

What can help you hold actual conversations is to . . .

◄ **1. Know how to conjugate the present tense of some verbs, beginning with "to be" and "to have."** ► These two are often irregular since through intensive use they get shortened and changed. And it definitely helps to learn to form **a past tense.**

Practice constructing simple sentences using pronouns, verbs, and adjectives. ◄ Say these out loud. ► (On the plane, speak out loud—to *yourself*, please.) It's obvious, but it helps to be reminded that once you have a particular "sentence model," you can plug in other words that you know.

2. Know how to form *questions*. E.g., "Have you . . ." or "Do you have . . ." Practice forming questions using "models."

3. Know how to form *negatives*. E.g., "I have no change" or "I am not here." (You could use this latter if someone you don't like is bothering you.) Practice forming negatives.

4. The importance of word order and word endings. Some languages depend heavily on word order to convey changes in sentence meaning; e.g., English and French. (People eat apples and Apples eat people.) Some depend much more on word endings; e.g., Russian. And many depend on both, e.g., German.

It can be hard for a native speaker to unravel a convoluted word order. Begin by learning to construct simple sentences like those suggested above. For example, "She is happy." "He does that." "You can come back tomorrow." "Does he have change?"

5. Learn the some basic word endings for subjects and objects, if the language you are learning requires it.

Try

People respond favorably when other people are really trying, no matter how imperfect the result. This is a good place to recall:

> **The Invincible Law of Human Achievement:** If one person can do it, then entire generations can do it — so *you* can do it.

"What is essential is invisible to the eye."
Antoine St. Exupery, *The Little Prince*

After you go through this, you may not be able to fix a sewing machine or a catapult, but you should have a better sense of the simple ideas that underlie mechanical movement.

The particular machines that we're talking about involve forces and motions connected with moving bodies and their direct physical contact—as opposed to electrical, chemical, or nuclear influences (which are not unrelated). The basic idea is that **all machines are trading devices.** Mechanical machines may either **(1)** bestow extra *force*, but take away some of the *distance* traveled (or extend the *time* required), or **(2)** cause something to gain more distance (or reduce the time required) at the expense of some force.

When you operate a crowbar, for example, the small force you apply is magnified at the other end, but you need to move your end much farther than the prying end moves. Got it? The opposite occurs when a golfer strikes a golf ball with a lot of power. The ball has less force but goes much farther than the club (one hopes).

How Machines Work—The Naming of Parts

Machines always involve two parts (or two aspects) that we'll call Part One (or **the effort**) and Part Two (**the weight**). Part One is what somebody or something moves directly, and Part Two is what moves as a result. In a crowbar, the end that you move is Part One, while the end that pries something up as a result of your effort is Part Two. Before you flee to the next paragraph (or chapter), please take a moment to realize how remarkable it must have seemed to the ancients for these two parts to be in one and the same object. For instance, when a wheel is rolling along, half of it is rotating in the opposite direction!

There is also Part Three, the Lazy Part.

The Law of Laziness: Nothing ever happens without something else involved that doesn't officially "do" anything.

In a **lever,** which is one of *the* really fundamental machines (the crowbar and seesaw are levers), the Lazy Part is the *fulcrum.* This is the part on which the other parts move (such as the middle of the seesaw where it's attached to the ground.) Everything depends upon the Lazy Part, the fulcrum, even though the fulcrum itself doesn't move and doesn't really care (at least professionally) which side is getting the better deal.

With an **inclined plane** or **wedge,** the Lazy Part is the ramp itself. The ramp doesn't do anything while the material is either being pushed up—or wedged up—its length. It just sits there. (I have to admit that these lazy parts are often supporting a lot of weight or doing something else critical to the enterprise. But in twentieth-century physics, an object that is just supporting weight isn't considered to be doing any "work"—e.g., you're standing there with big bags of groceries waiting for someone to open the door, so you're not officially "working." I'm sorry, you can tell it to your arms, but that's the way it is.)

In a **wheel and axle** (another basic machine), the Lazy Part is the center point, which doesn't rotate! (This is more strange than we think.)

The other two basic machines are the **pulley** (a kind of lever) and the **screw** (an inclined plane wrapped around a wheel and axle, a nifty idea that endlessly impressed Archimedes).

Looking at the lever, we observe the important fact that a lever—e.g., a seesaw—rotates in a *circular arc*. (Think about that for a moment.) Both the wheel and axle, and the pulley, are simply levers that, rotating; *traverse the entire circle*. So all of these machines derive from a circular rotation.

Some Interesting Examples

Lever. Oars, shovels, scissors, fishing poles, throwing (or batting) arms, wheelbarrows, doors(!).
Wedge. Knives.
Wheel and Axle. Screwdrivers.

◆ Basic Medical Supplies ◆

I wouldn't presume to tell readers what items are good to have on hand for common medical emergencies without taking an extensive survey of doctors, pharmacists, and concerned parents. Brand names are specified in some cases, but (as is the case throughout this book) this doesn't mean there aren't other products or methods *just as good*.

DISINFECTANTS
(Wash cuts carefully with soap and water.)

1. Betadine—excellent all-purpose disinfectant for simple as well as serious wounds. Looks orange, washes out.

2. Neosporin or Polysporin—for the usual cuts and scrapes.

TOOLS

1. Cotton swabs—e.g., Q-tips. To keep these as germ-free as possible (Q-tips are not sterile), after removing the outer plastic wrap, do not do what Q-tips tells you to do, which is to puncture the smaller plastic covering in the center for "easier removal." This will expose the swabs ever after to the air. Instead, slide the box in and out of its sleeve.

2. Scissors, tweezers, thermometer.

BANDAGES

1. Little ones, medium ones, and large ones.

2. Individually wrapped gauze pads.

3. You can improvise a splint with tightly wrapped newspaper and hold it on with a towel.

EMERGENCY PHONE NUMBERS

1. In most areas the phone number for *any* genuine emergency is 911.

2. Poison Control—there is a number in your phone book.

Other Helpful Items that May Be
— Essential for You or Your Family —

FEVERS, HEADACHES
Aspirin and Tylenol (children under the age of five shouldn't take aspirin).

SUN PROTECTION
1. Sunscreen—appropriate for your complexion type. SPF (Sun-Protection Factor) 15 is supposed to be sufficient to block unwanted rays.
2. Solarcaine—for sunburn.

STOMACH
Alka-Seltzer or Pepto-Bismol—for upset stomach.

EYES
To remove a tiny particle, rinse in cool water.

FEMININE
Gyne-Lotrimin or Monistat.

SKIN
Calamine lotion (insect bites, poison ivy, poison oak). An old-fashioned remedy that helps.

CANKER SORES
Campho-Phenique or Ambesol (especially the gel)—put on the sore at night (applied locally inside mouth is okay), possibly gone in the morning.

SPLINTER REMOVAL

Hydrogen peroxide, then use a pin that has been sterilized with flame and alcohol. Tweezers are generally a second choice (usually not fine enough). (Hydrogen peroxide is remarkably effective for washing out bloodstains on clothing.)

ALCOHOL

For cleaning implements.

CHICKEN SOUP

Genuine medical researchers have determined that chicken soup is very good for you. "Chicken soup is a well-recognized and widely used treatment for a variety of illnesses."*

◆ Metric Conversions and the Acre ◆

"And kilometers to go before I sleep.
And kilometers to go before I sleep."
Robert Frost in pain

The Unknown Acre

Do you realize that even though the size of an **acre** is quite important (e.g., you may need to apply it to the size of some real estate), no one ever told you *in practical terms* how large an acre is? Maybe they told you there are 640 acres in a square mile, or that an acre is 43,560 square feet. So what? This may be useful for accounting purposes but not for your eye or your judgment.

* *New England Journal of Medicine*, October 21, 1985, pg. 161.

AN ACRE IS ABOUT 70 YARDS ON A SIDE—I.E., ABOUT TWO-THIRDS OF THE LENGTH OF A FOOTBALL FIELD.

Basic Metrics

Since most readers will have little interest in converting anything *to* a metric measurement, "basic" is limited here to converting metric to English, the standard U.S. system.

$$1 \text{ centimeter} = \text{ }^2/_5 \text{ in. (.4 in.)}$$
$$1 \text{ meter (m.)} = 39.37 \text{ in. (about 1 yd. 3 in.)}$$
$$\blacktriangleleft \text{ } 1 \text{ kilometer (km.)} = \text{ }^5/_8 \text{ mi. } \blacktriangleright$$
$$1 \text{ kilogram (kg.)} = 2.2 \text{ lbs. (about 2 lbs., 3 oz.)}$$

That's all.*

Optional (or Is It?)

I would like to convey the following "arguments" to the metric enthusiast, defined here as someone who wishes—for some odd reason, often with unrestrained vehemence—to replace in daily life our standard system of measurement with the metric system. I ask only that the reader reflect soberly on the following arguments before continuing this (misguided) crusade:

THE ARGUMENT FROM GENUINE COMMON SENSE
Inches, feet, yards, etc., arose out of practical and sensible activities, and thus these lengths conform to our real perceptions more precisely than those of the metric system, which *were designed artificially*.

---

* Most people rarely need to convert liters to quarts anymore, but just in case, a liter is slightly more than a quart.

It is difficult to dispute the superior elegance and efficiency of the metric system in the service of science, but in our daily lives it is quite the opposite. Take, for example, centimeters, which are used to measure someone's height in metric. A centimeter is less than half an inch. It is clearly too small a measurement. To say that someone is 185 centimeters tall is ridiculous. To most normally alive people, this doesn't need to be explained; it's obvious. It needs explaining only to those who don't get it.* Possibly the idea of imposing the metric system was initiated by fatigued European hikers who preferred, quite understandably, to come upon a sign saying, 4 KM. TO LODGE instead of 4 MI. TO LODGE.†

THE ARGUMENT FROM POETRY

A primary component of poetry—not to mention all conversations between people—is sensitivity to *connotation*. Now, in our modern science, connotation is at best very dubious. It may contribute to the intuitive leap to a possible truth, but for testing and measuring it isn't very useful. And yet *in our daily lives* it is quite the opposite. For example, an inch, a foot, a yard, a mile bring forth an entire cultural heritage. For instance, "a country mile" has a meaning far beyond the literal, just as ". . . wider than a mile."‡ (You might try substituting "kilometer" in the above.) *Mile* is a spacious— and powerful—word that calls up a substantial distance, and while *kilometer* is an elegant mathematical and scientific word, it connotates something quite different. *Mile* was created to express a distance that took a worthwhile effort to

* Decimeters, about 4 inches long, are rarely used in ordinary life by those countries that employ metric. Why? It's too boring a notion.
† The fact that many European countries employ the metric system means nothing. People are capable of accepting almost anything, and after a while real values get buried and forgotten.
‡ From the song "Moon River," words by Johnny Mercer, music by Henry Mancini.

span—an "open" word. *Kilometer* (in daily life) is a word that replaces the sense of length with that of a distance to ride over. To some, it sounds like clackety gear wheels. *Kilometer* has its place, but not at the expense of a word we can't afford to lose. It's like saying farewell to all of the eagles.

To eliminate a word, in fact, an entire *concept* such as "mile"—one that at times can even touch us profoundly—is going too far. One has the privilege of not believing this, but to impose that denial on the rest of us who may experience something of value (an experience available to everyone) is really not reasonable; in fact, it is narrow-minded by any standard.

◆ The Law of Neckties ◆

Let's face it. Ties are kind of weird. No doubt they were inspired by some kind of male insecurity, but now they are often the most colorful items men wear (women wear them too, sometimes). However, you would have to contort reality quite a bit to describe how useful a tie is. Quite the opposite. For example, it is well-known that ties *attract* liquid and food substances of every kind. In fact, there is . . .

The First Law of Neckties: The first time you wear a new necktie, the chances you will spill food or liquid on it are twelve out of seventeen.

But since ties are indispensable in many domains of modern reality, here are the necessary instructions:

How to Tie a Necktie ____
(Four-in-Hand and Windsor)

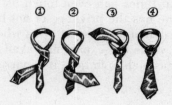

THE FOUR-IN-HAND

This is the most common knot. It is simple to tie, but getting the length right may require more than one try if it's an unfamiliar tie. (The length of the front part that shows should come down just to the belt buckle, and above all it has to cover comfortably the flap underneath.)

1. Wrap the working end of the tie *(the fat end)* **a** *full turn and a half* **around the standing part** *(the skinny end)*—which is the part that just stays there doing nothing in particular.

2. Bring the working end up through the large loop formed, then tuck it down through the small loop in front, as shown.

3. To tighten, hold the standing part with one hand; with the other, pull down on the working end, then push up on the knot itself. For utter correctness (optional nowadays), you can "dimple" the tie, i.e., by pushing in the bottom of the knot after it's pulled tight.

THE WINDSOR

This is another well-known knot. It is tied exactly like the four-in-hand except that you **begin by tying an Overhand Knot.** (More precisely, it's a *Half-Hitch*, as described on pg. 114, but you don't need to know this.) The extra turn makes the Windsor a larger, broader knot.

THE BOW TIE

I would have said that unless you are a certain vanishing breed of *aficionado*, you should purchase a permanently tied bow tie and clip it on. But those who have strong feelings about the bow tie are understandably offended at this callous disregard for a genuine tradition. To them, these two kinds of bow ties—the clip-on and the real—are as different as Nevada and East Coast bagels. Do what you need to do and don't let me know about it.

Tie Patterns

These appear to fall into five very general categories: (1) solids, (2) stripes, (3) small allover patterns, such as dots, little amoebas, geometrically shaped amoebas, etc., (4) paisley-style designs, i.e., large amoebas with swirls, (5) originals, often larger allover patterns or intensive extensions of paisley-style designs, and, finally, (6) joke ties.

Fashions change, but you don't have to. Small allover patterns are perennially good; so are tasteful paisleys.

How to Iron a Tie

WITH NORMAL EQUIPMENT

You never have to send your tie out for pressing. Place a

slightly damp towel over the tie and apply the iron over the towel to press out wrinkles.

WITH ABNORMAL EQUIPMENT
In an emergency, without an iron, you can use what's known as the "boardinghouse iron." Turn on a lamp. When the bulb is hot, cover your hand with a handkerchief, unscrew the hot bulb, quickly put the bulb inside of a sock and iron out those wrinkles. *Test first with a joke tie.*

——— *The Second Law of Neckties* ———

People who wear ties almost always have huge numbers of them, ranging from the utterly boring to the utterly bizarre. *The Second Law of Neckties* assures us that at least two of these ties are *never worn*.

◆ How to Check the Water and Oil, ◆ and Pump Gas

In the good old days (gone forever), a pleasant service station attendant filled your tank (you didn't have a choice)—and checked your water and oil.* But now if you fill your own, no one checks these for you. You're supposed to inspect the level of these vital fluids at least every other fill-up. So you have to decide how you're going to manage. Your car's life span may depend on your decision.

---

* Here "water" is an automobile code word for antifreeze and sometimes even for water itself.

142

A Handy Tip

◄ Keep a single glove in your car. ► This "car-hand" can be a cast-off leather glove or other tough substance—an old work glove or stained dress glove will do nicely. The car-hand is *guaranteed* to make your life more pleasant (and possibly more extended).

Fluid Adventures

Since checking the water and oil is easy and takes less than a minute, my main concern is to keep horrible grime off your body and your clothing.

First, locate the following three items under your hood:* *the oil dipstick, the oil cap, and the radiator cap.*

Put on Your Car-Hand When You — Check the Water and Oil —

CHECKING THE WATER

1. Wear your car-hand. (The radiator cap is possibly hot.)

2. Open the radiator cap *slowly.* This is a normal precaution in case the car is overheating. The liquid in the radiator should come up to an inch or so from the top, but it's not that precise. NOTE: On most new cars you don't add liquid via the radiator cap—you add it to a secondary (plastic) reservoir alongside.

3. If you need just a little liquid, add water. If you need a lot—and you've been having your radiator checked

* If necessary, use the manual—or ask. *Just be sure.*

frequently—add antifreeze or water and have your mechanic check it out.

4. Screw on the cap and close the hood. So far, your car-hand has protected you from possible heat and steam. It gets better:

CHECKING THE OIL

Oil comes in "weights" that consist of one or two numbers; for example, 10-40, 20-50, or 30. Roughly speaking, the colder the weather, the lower the numbers, the thinner the oil. But all you need to know is *what weight oil is in your car now.*

1. Drive your car at least fifteen minutes, stop, and turn off the engine.

2. Pull out the *dipstick*—a long, thin piece of flimsy metal.

3. Wipe the oil off the stick. (You can use the paper towels supplied by the gas station.)

4. Slide the stick *all the way down* into its slit.

5. Pull the stick out again and note the level of oil on the bottom of the stick. If it lies *above the "low" mark*, reinsert the stick and do nothing. If it reaches *only the "low" mark*, you must *add one quart of the weight of the oil you are now using.* (If it comes up only to the mark below that, add two quarts—though you should never let your car need more than a single quart.) If you don't know what the weight is already in your engine, just add 10-40, and the next time you have an oil change, find out what is used.

6. To add oil, unscrew the oil cap and pour in the oil. Screw the oil cap back on pretty tight. Note that your car-hand will now have kept horrible grime away. But it gets even better, and more important.

Put on Your Car-Hand When You Pump Gas—Life-Extension Practice

KNOW YOUR OCTANE

If your car takes unleaded fuel (it probably does), *never use leaded gasoline.*

1. Unscrew your gas cap and put it somewhere obvious.

2. Lift up the nozzle from its holder and push up on the holder. (On some pumps, you have to push a lever down or press a button.)

3. Insert the end of the nozzle as far into your tank as it goes, and squeeze the handle toward you. Now listen to this:

4. If there is a locking catch on the nozzle so that you can insert it and it will pump—and stop—automatically, **walk away from the pump and get some fresh air.** The side of the gas tank has various instructions about staying away from gas, which I won't ruin your day by quoting. But you get the idea.

Always wear your car-hand when you pump gas. Not only for health reasons,* but for smell reasons (gasoline tends to remain permanently on human skin, and if you drive with your hand at the top of the wheel, the gas will be about six to ten inches from your nose).

---

* As far as service station attendants are concerned, it is possible that, just like the utilities people, they may escape ill effects because they, too, are *athletes of gas* (see pg. 160).

◆ Difficult Openings ◆

"Open Coriander!!"
Ali Baba (false start)

Easy (Not Irritating)

The jar won't open. Two classical procedures, and one non-historical procedure.

1. The Brute Method. (Perhaps the smartest and quickest of all.) Ask someone nearby who is stronger.

2. The Invincible Method. Holding a dishtowel in your hand, apply hot water around the lid. The lid expands slightly (also sticky particles dissolve). Unscrew immediately.

3. The Most Amazing Method Since the Creation of Jars. There is no reason that you should believe this until you actually succeed with it. When an occasion arises, remember this as a worthwhile experiment. You can always fall back on the graceless "Invincible Method"—"invincible" because it brings to bear on the poor jar an entire plumbing and heating technology.

This method asks you simply to open the jar. It's no big production. This method *truly is amazing*, but not easy—it's almost impossible—to describe! Don't try to bring any zealous, excessive force. You need no other effort than to relax your arm and shoulder, put your hand on the lid, and not think about how to open the jar. Let your body take over. The more you relax, the easier it is. *Don't think about how you're going to do it; in fact, deliberately distract your mind*

146

from trying to help. What was that song you were trying to remember? Is it raining out, or what? Where will you go on your next vacation? IT OPENED! HOW DID IT DO THAT?

This method suggests that our hands and our bodies know more about opening jars than our heads. In a way, it's not quite as easy as it sounds, yet there comes a moment . . . when it works! This is absolutely a fact. (But a weird fact.)

——— *Harder (Rage-Producing)* ———

You buy almost anything wrapped in plastic. Unless you're Wolfman—or Wolfwoman—how do you strip off the covering? It's horrible and it's getting worse. In fact, I have in front of me an object that is so wrapped, it even has an *arrow* with the word *open* underneath. But it points to nothing. It just sits there, as if everybody died and the traffic lights are still changing.

Another mean device of these pitiless manufacturers is to have a very simple way of extruding the desired item from its cell, but not telling you what it is. So after you have torn your nails, searched for a jabbing implement to puncture the J. Edgar Hoover–like insulation, and then butchered the package—almost killing its now-frightened occupant—you discern that if you press a certain secret place, often on the rear of the package, the object will step out just like Fred Astaire.

What to do?

1. Study the package for clues.

2. From your—usually bitter—experience, try to distinguish false clues from real clues.

3. Have a jabber handy—nail clippers, a nail (not yours), a pushpin or jewelry pin, the prong of your belt buckle!

TIP: For those plastic grocery and garbage bags that don't tell you which edge is the "open" edge, **moisten your fingers before checking out the edges.**

___ *Hardest (Beyond the Range of* ___ *Human Emotions)*

The sardine can won't open. You messed up using the absurd little "key" that comes with every can. Actually, you've managed to roll back some of the can, but if you keep mashing it around, you'll probably get greasy metal in your fish (ugh!). Here's what to do:

1. **Pour out the oil.**
2. **Change your menu to sardine pressé.**
3. **Use a can opener at the other end, and open up the top as far as possible** without getting greasy metal into the fish (ugh!).
4. **Try to extricate the sardines with a fork** (usually easier than with a knife or spoon). It may or may not work.
5. **Use pliers,** and videotape the event for possible future litigation.

◆ How to Pack a Suitcase ◆

In our time: **(1)** Aspirin works and nobody knows precisely why; **(2)** there's a certain something about an attractive hat, but nobody really knows what; and **(3)** in a garment bag, placing individual plastic covers from the cleaners over your suits, blouses, shirts, skirts, etc., prevents their wrinkling and nobody knows exactly how.

The First Law of Epochs: Each has its own humbling inventory of unexplained knowledge.

Garment Bags

If you travel even a modest amount, I strongly recommend a garment bag, a brilliant invention. (Clothes on hangers will come out looking fresher.)

1. Don't pack the bag too full. Keep it light so you can carry and stow it easily.

2. Hang your toughest garment closest to the side of the bag's "fold." Items placed there get the most abuse.

Regular Bags—Hard vs. Soft

News from the front: Hard bags are losing. It's true that a hard bag doesn't get punctured, it doesn't get wet inside if it falls into a puddle, and its contents come out less wrinkled. Yet more people prefer soft bags. A soft bag is lighter, more comfortable under an airplane seat, and if packed properly, its contents supposedly come out just as wrinkle-free.*

Rolling Up, the Core of Packing

Of course, there are umpteen ways to pack up, but no matter how you do it, an assortment of plastic bags is very useful.

* If you buy "soft," purchase one of at least intermediate quality. (Take my word for this.)

149

You've heard about "rolling up" and maybe you've tried it. But even though rolling is easy on your clothes and didn't require tissue paper or complicated folding, it didn't work for you. Why? Because you did it backward. Try it this way:

1. Clothing that doesn't wrinkle easily, or on which a few wrinkles don't matter (like blue jeans), are rolled *first*. This will be the soft/lumpy core of a roll. Each roll may contain at least three or four layers.

2. Around the core, roll up the more delicate items—the sweaters, the blouses, etc. You can roll them up together or one at a time. Sweaters and blouses get their arms folded in before rolling. It doesn't matter which end you start rolling on as long as *the more delicate articles are rolled up LAST*.

3. Put the roll inside a plastic bag—especially if the outside garments are delicate. If the bag is a large one, tie a knot in it so that it's reasonably tight around the roll. Place the rolls on or near the bottom of your suitcase.

Other

Heavy and awkward objects should be placed in the separate compartments in your bag—shoes, the lowest down (away from the handle). Stuff shoes with socks and put them in a plastic bag.* Also, your belts will last longer if you don't coil them up; instead, circle them around the other items.

Put socks, underwear, and other homogeneous collections of articles in individual plastic bags and stuff them in between other items to help keep the contents from shifting. (Having everything conveniently sorted also enables you, if need be, to live more comfortably out of your suitcase.)

---

* Or in a "shoe bag." This is a cloth bag with a pull string that you can find for a few dollars in some shoe stores.

CAUTION: Liquids such as shampoo or lotions expand under low pressure—e.g., on an airplane. Practically speaking, this means that unless the bottles are new and unopened, they should be no more than three-quarters full, placed in a plastic bag, and put in a carry-on or a compartment with other nondelicate items.

━━━━━━━━ *Optional* ━━━━━━━━

It's nice to have wheels on your bags. This is better than a fold-up dolly since that just means another object to stow somewhere on an airplane. But if you get one of these dollies for a present, don't complain.

◆ How to Paint a Room ◆

The ornamentation of walls has been going on at least since the production of cave pictures. So what will folks like us be covering up the walls and ceilings of their living quarters with in the year 3000? (Of course, it might be caves all over again. . . .)

"Hey, Rorg, pass me the light spread—the $6c^5h^4/d$. I'm doing an ancient twenty-third-century Mustang transparency up in this corner. Boy, it's musty. Here, let me stand on your shoulder."

"What about ladders?"

"What's a ladder?"

"I saw one in a dreamOgraph. Very complicated. It had holes in it that you stepped into. Looked like somebody was using this thing to reach up, but I couldn't figure out how they did it with all those holes."

"Sounds weird. Makes my head ache just thinking about it. Hey, don't wiggle while I'm up here!"

There are strange pockets in the world of space-time.

Preparation—For Twentieth/ Twenty-first-Century Painting

PREPARATION IS MORE THAN HALF THE JOB

1. Wash everything. Be especially unmerciful with kitchens and bathrooms.

2. If there are small cracks and holes in the walls, fill them with spackle (plaster filler—available at any hardware store), using a putty knife. When it's dry, sand lightly and wipe away the dust. Nothing seems easier to do, but this *is* a more delicate job than it appears. By the way, it is almost impossible to smooth these patches with your fingers.

3. Use a screwdriver to remove the hardware: doorknob plates, outlet-switch plates, window locks.

The Painting

The Law of Painting: Always try to paint with someone—it's fun, it goes five times faster, and you work up an appetite.

I assume that you are going to use latex (water-base) paint, which now comes in flat, semigloss, and enamel. Unless you're a pro (in which case you don't need me) this is the only way to go. You can wash everything up with soap and warm water.

1. **Use flat paint for ceilings and walls, and semi-gloss for doors, trim, kitchen, and bathroom.** Over a light color, one coat may be enough (look at it *when dry*). Trim may take an additional coat.

2. **Be sure the undercoat is dry before applying the second coat. To test, run your fingernail over the surface: if paint comes off on your nail, it's not dry.** NOTE: The second coat goes on much easier than the first.

3. **Try to obtain sufficient paint to finish a complete coat.** Two color matches never look exactly the same. An average room takes two gallons of paint; the trim, a quart. Get it all at once. If you have some extra left over, save for later touch-ups.

4. **Get a 2-inch nylon brush for the edges where rollers can't reach, and a 2-inch nylon angled sash brush for the trim** (try painting the trim with and without this brush and you'll know exactly why you bought it).

5. **Paint from the top down.** Start with the ceiling, edging it first where it meets the wall. Then edge the wall where it meets the ceiling, and so on. Finish with the trim.

PAINTING WITH BRUSHES

1. **Dip the brush into a pail that's half-full.** (Don't risk spills.) As you lift the brush, some paint will drip off.

2. **Slap the brush a couple of times against both sides of the pail.** (You will feel like a real painter.) Never slide the brush over the pail's edge.

PAINTING WITH ROLLERS

1. **Soak the roller in a pan that's about two-thirds**

full—and pull it up. The roller will be full of paint, but it won't drip. Everybody rolls in different directions, and it all works. Let the mad adherents (see pg. 98) contradict themselves about *their* superior methods, and go on painting. But it does help to start each sequence away from the previously rolled one. You can make the last roll a slightly "feathered" stroke overlapping into the previous area.

Spills. Always have a damp cloth on your person to immediately wipe off paint splatters. If you get these right away, it's not a problem. For large spills, use newspaper.

Essential Extras

A wooden stir stick and a cap (unless you enjoy washing paint out of your hair)—from the paint store.

A drop cloth, lots of newspapers—you can use layers of them to cover areas the drop cloths don't.

A razor blade or scraper—use to get paint off windows.

Masking tape or "painter's tape"—from the paint store. Using tape to mask depends on the steadiness of your hand. If you have wood paneling, definitely mask it.

Painting clothes. When you paint you not only get to wear *really old clothes*, you get to wear *REALLY OLD WEIRD CLOTHES* and *GET AWAY WITH IT* as long as they cover you (e.g., elf clothing, pirate clothing, abominable clothing, clothing your Aunt Boris gave you, etc.).

How to Park Your Car

The subject is *parallel parking*, which causes enough tension—especially before someone's first driving test—to support pharmaceutical companies.

Directions are given only for parking on the right side of the street, since being able to park on the left of a (one-way) street is even easier.

Preparation

1. The parking space has to be longer than your car—at least four feet, and even better, five feet. (You should always leave enough room for the cars parked in front and behind to exit easily.) This means you have to be able to estimate this distance quickly. For reasons we can't entirely explain, humans can do this right away.

2. When you find a parking spot, signal the traffic behind you by activating your brake lights and turn signal. As you begin to park, make sure that no car is passing you, since at the start of your maneuver, the front of your car will jut out into the traffic lane.

DEFINITIONS

The car parked in front of you is the *forward car;* the car behind is the *rear car.*

The following is an overview of the basics. We'll look at some of the crucial details just after.

1. Pull up *two to three feet from the forward car* so that both vehicles have their rear bumpers more or less lined up. If the space is quite generous, you can afford to have your rear bumper as much as two feet *behind* the forward car's rear bumper, which makes parking a walk in the park.

2. Turn your steering wheel steadily to the right as you back slowly into the space. Don't let your car assume more than a *45° angle* (half a right angle) as you back in.

3. For average-size and larger cars, *at a certain point straighten your wheels* as you continue backing. For some small cars, this may not be necessary.

4. When your front bumper is even with the rear bumper of the forward car, quickly turn the steering wheel all the way to the left and continue backing slowly in. This is fairly obvious, but some people can't restrain themselves from turning left too soon and end up scraping the forward car.

5. Before touching the rear car, move forward slowly, turning your wheel to the right so that you are parallel to the curb and centered in the space. If the parking place is very tight, you may need to go backward and forward a few times, turning the wheel to the right and then left while backing, then once again following Step 5—until the car is properly positioned in the space. Please don't bump into the rear car.

For some readers, it is important to state that Steps 1–4 explain the "generic" parking sequence. Of course, as you become more experienced, this all seems a little stilted.

— *Lining Up, and Straightening Up* —

As usual with life activities, the crucial actions are not necessarily the obvious ones. Most mistakes seem to occur while **lining up** (Step 1) and **straightening your wheels** (Step 3). Everything else depends on these two.

LINING UP

The problem is that not all cars are the same width. If you think about this for a moment, you will see that in a way the forward car is a (large) red herring. The only important thing about that car is—*don't hit it*. What's important initially is how far *your* car is from the *curb*. That's why if you position an average-size car two feet from a much narrower forward car, you will have to be much more accurate to avoid hitting the curb when you first back into the space. (I see nods of heads.)

Much easier is the following: Whatever size your car is, if the forward car is more or less similar in width, then use the general two-to-three-foot rule.

6. But if your car is a good deal wider than the forward car, then three feet should be the minimum distance; if a good deal narrower, then two feet will make parking easier. If you end up too far from the curb, you may be starting too far from the forward car.

STRAIGHTENING UP

This is where it's a hundred times better if your "body"

takes over, which fortunately happens after you have parked x number of times. Try straightening your wheels when your front door is alongside the rear bumper of the forward car.

If you hit the curb going back, you went past the 45° angle or straightened out too late—or both.

NOTE: Just because your body is going to eventually take over a lot of the details of this maneuver, you will still need to pay attention.

◆ How to Sharpen a Pencil on a ◆ Piece of Sandpaper or a Knife

This is useful if you're trying to mark accurate perpendicular lines on wood for cutting and you are nowhere near a pencil sharpener, or perhaps you are out in the country sketching.

I have seen people rubbing pencils furiously back and forth on sandpaper, or rotating these generally unheralded servants of culture and communication across the sandy grit in wild, unsatisfying scrapings to try to obtain a nice point. With sandpaper, you can end up with a boring, blunt lead.

And I have seen the knife people carve up the leads of pencils only to be utterly aggravated by stubby—or even fractured—points.

How to Do It

SANDPAPER
Lay the pencil on the sandpaper, then twirl it with your

thumb and index finger while moving it toward you. Keep repeating until the point comes fine.

KNIFE
Expose the lead in the usual way—by slicing off some wood all around—but then only work at the *tip* of the lead, down to about $1/16''$ or slightly more. Use the edge of the knife like sandpaper, delicately scraping it back and forth while you rotate the pencil with your other hand.

◆   How to Light a Pilot Light   ◆

We're talking GAS here, so look alert.

1. IF THERE'S A LOT OF GAS IN THE AIR (i.e., if it smells), it is dangerous because
   · It can kill you.
   · It can catch on fire, which often has bad consequences.

2. Do not light anything. Immediately open windows and doors.

3. Call the utility company or your plumber.

4. Turn off your main gas line.

You must absolutely know how to turn off your main gas line. Find it. It consists of either a large knob to be TURNED OFF (clockwise) or a large nut to be SHUT OFF (clockwise—use a pipe wrench, much easier to apply here than pliers). If it's a nut, and especially if you live in an earthquake zone, **attach a pipe wrench to the nut and leave it there,** or attach *channel locks,* a combination pliers and wrench that opens up very wide. Great for pipes.

159

This way, if you suddenly have to turn off the gas, you won't have to fumble for a wrench in possible darkness.

1. **VERY SMALL GAS LEAKS should be attended to immediately.** They are often caused by a pilot light on the stove going out.

2. **Open all the windows.**

3. **Locate the pilot lights on your stove.** Stoves are different, but not that different: Lift up the top of your stove as if you were going to clean it. You will probably see the pilot lights for the other burners.

4. **If a pilot light is unlit, hold a lighted match at the place of the missing flame.** Once lit, if the flame looks weaker than the others, then look nearby for a small *adjusting screw*. To increase the flame, open up the screw (by turning it slightly to the left, counterclockwise). To reduce the flame, do the opposite.

5. **If you have a recurring problem, call the utility company.**

Other Appliances

What if the pilot goes out in the water heater—or the gas furnace? No problem. Next to the pilot light on these larger appliances will be *instructions*. (Are you as amazed as I am?) Often these instructions tell you to push down a button for a long time before you do anything else. It's weird, but just do exactly what they say.

The Athletes of Gas

Utility persons. These are men and women who will (actually!) come to your house, like an old-fashioned doctor making a house call. These folks tend to be very polite and professional and, of course, know their jobs very well.

But if you should happen to be one of those people who is very sensitive to minute amounts of gas, you will discover that the utility persons invariably won't believe you when you say you still smell gas (and they don't). This is not their fault. *They are athletes of gas!* They can survive in exotic atmospheres in which you and I would shrivel up. Persevere politely and they will generally do all they can to help detect the leak—if there actually is one.

◆ The Plumbing System ◆

"$E = mc^2$"

Albert Einstein, an honorary member of the Plumbers Union*

What happens to all the stuff that you don't want to know what happens to?

How It Happens

There's a big pipe (appropriately named a "soil stack") that runs up and down in our houses and apartments. The drainpipes from sinks, tubs, showers, toilets, appliances, etc., are tilted slightly downward so that gravity pulls the mostly liquid waste into the soil stack and into the community sewer

---

* He really was. Einstein was fascinated by a plumber's capacity to visualize and work in three dimensions.

pipe, then ever onward to a treatment plant, where very humane bacteria are diligently breaking down the . . . You don't really want to know what goes on in there, do you? (You can call up the treatment plant and ask.)

A private means of getting rid of sewage is through a septic tank, where other even more humane bacteria are encouraged to . . . (You get the idea.) The waste is ultimately decomposed into units that Nature prefers to deal with, and it disappears (one hopes) into a "disposal" field, where unbelievably it helps things grow.

Traps and Vents—Important Secondary Features

TRAPS

A brilliant yet simple idea. Traps are nothing more than U-shaped bends in drainpipes. Since the bottom of the "U" is lower than the neighboring portions it will *retain water*. Thus, it acts as a *seal* to stop gases and even little nasty creatures (for whom sewage is something pleasant) from getting from one side of the "U" (the sewer) to the other side (your home).

VENTS

Needed because sewage produces gas, which is released through a vent in your roof by means of a series of pipes (called—can you believe it?—"vent pipes"), which are connected to the drainpipes.

Optional

Just in case you don't know this, fresh water enters your home under pressure, and at the hot-water heater it divides into two independent streams—cold and hot. Pressure forces these streams up to where you request them—by turning on a faucet. (Don't be anxious. The incoming water system is totally separate from the waste system.)

Though most toilets and sinks have individual shutoff valves right underneath them, in case of emergencies you should know where the *Main Shutoff* is in your home. Invariably, it is near the water meter or where the water main enters the house.

The Law of Water: All of our water originates in the sky.

Yes, it all comes down as rain.

Getting to the Next Plateau of Pocket Billiards

Certain sports, e.g., baseball and billiards, have achieved a kind of mathematical and theatrical perfection.

Pocket billiards, or pool,* is a game of endless nonrepetition and pure truth. Even the *sounds* that billiard balls make are elegant. However, achieving that elegance in your shooting skill is another matter. You are finally about to learn why so many of your shots never went in and why most of your position play never worked.

But before we move on to straight pool, so to speak, it's important to understand the fundamental principle of the Science of Ignorance: More genuine knowledge leads to a greater realization of what we don't know. For example:

The Law of Pool: Unless you acquire new knowledge, you will at most play at the upper level of the lowest plateau.

* "Three-cushion billiards" (no pockets) is probably the "purest" billiard game played today, but it is not as popular as pocket billiards.

164

You will not even recognize what another player does to play on a higher plateau. As a further incentive, remember that only a knowledgeable opponent can appreciate your brilliant and subtle successes (and failures).

I assume that you know the fundamentals of play, holding the cue and all that. But a couple of points should be emphasized:

1. *Follow through,* **keeping the cue as level as possible.** Do not pull or snap back. (In some close situations you will have to remove your cue quickly. But complete follow-through is the principle to work from.)

2. On every shot, after chalking the cue, you must balance the three fundamental factors: *direction,* *speed,* **and** *spin.* Most players know enough about direction.* They are frequently confused, unknowingly, about the effects of spin. And the significance of speed, to first-plateau players, is almost completely unknown.

_____ *Speed, or, Leave Your Physics* _____ *Teacher in the Dust*

Welcome to the Looking-Glass World of BILLIARD-BALL SPEED. That's right, you're in a world that makes no sense —until you realize that billiard balls, cloth, and chalked, poking implements create unexpected results. For example, the angles that a billiard ball makes on hitting and rebounding from a "cushion" are generally not equal because cushions are made of a strange galactic material (for instance, their "squish" factor doesn't correspond to any known sofa).

---

* When stroking the cue, keep your eye on either the *object ball* (preferred by most) or the *cue ball* (a few players, some great, do this)—but make up your mind which it will be.

165

Amazingly, speed, all by itself, affects not only the distance but the *path* of the cue ball after it strikes either an object ball or a rail.

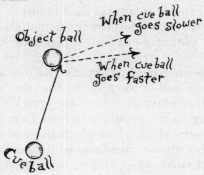

3. Very Important Speed Fact: To increase the immediate effect of spin, shoot softly. The faster the speed, the less immediate effect any spin will have that is imparted to the cue ball (i.e., side, top, or bottom spin).

4. Outrageous Speed Fact: The faster the speed, the less (or shallower) the angle at which the cue ball moves away from the object ball or the rail—i.e., it comes off *closer to you*. Thus, the *slower* the speed, the *greater* the angle the cue ball takes, moving farther away from you.

We've looked at these effects over and over, but did we ever actually *see* them? (Worth thinking about.)

Spin

I don't want to overburden you, but with the following facts about spin (presented to get you interested), and with more facts that you will eventually learn along with (some years of) practice, you will finally start making all kinds of shots you couldn't make before: extraordinary carom shots, impossible bank shots, stunning combinations, etc.

You already know that there is "follow" (topspin) and "draw" (bottom spin), which cause the cue ball to either continue its forward motion (follow) or move backward after striking an object ball (draw).

You also know about right and left "English" (i.e., right and left sidespin), which causes a ball to move more to the right or left after striking a rail. These four spins are effected, respectively, by stroking the cue ball no more than a cue tip's width above, below, to the right, or to the left of center. (For "big" draw, you can experiment with stroking the cue farther below the center than usually recommended. Follow through.)

5. First English Fact: Reverse English also slows the cue ball coming off the rail. I'm sure that you already know that "running" English on the cue ball (i.e., sidespin in the direction of its movement off a rail—often with the addition of topspin) will make a cue ball jump off a rail *faster and at a wider angle*. And "reverse" English (on the side of the cue ball opposite to its movement off a rail) will make the cue ball bounce off *slower and at a shallower angle*—even *backward* if enough English is applied (which is astounding to the uninitiated).

6. Second English Fact: English (sidespin) on the cue ball causes the initial path of the cue ball before it hits anything to curve in the direction of the English. E.g., right English makes the cue ball curve right. This is not an outrageous fact. It's the same principle as a curve in baseball (which is still fairly weird). **Also, the greater the velocity, the farther away the curvature begins to take effect** (this makes sense).

7. Third English Fact: English on the cue ball imparts the *opposite* English on the object ball. Now, this is reasonable, because you can put two balls next to each other, rotate one, and the other will rotate the opposite way. The spin imparted to the object ball is not as great, but it will slightly affect its path. ◄ However, if the object ball strikes a rail, the effect is pronounced. ► You, yourself, can easily test this, just as you can test all of the other items mentioned here.

NOTE: Once players understand and practice the above principles, they don't "figure" out, mentally, numerical angles or anything like that. ◄ By knowing the "secrets" and by practicing, your body can make the proper assessments —exactly as it does when you throw a ball right into someone's hands. ►

——— *Two Fundamental Principles* ———

LEARN TO PLAY "POSITION"

You cannot begin to advance to the next plateau—i.e., to begin to appreciate the full dimension of the game—without a serious study of position play. To practice playing position or "getting shape" (i.e., placing the cue ball where you wish to set up the next shot), ◄ select a moderate-size region where you wish the cue ball to end up. ► Use follow or draw (much more than English), gauge the speed, and practice.

8. It is easier to control the path of the cue ball with *follow* rather than with *draw*—a good point to keep in mind.

9. *THE MOST IMPORTANT FACT* about spin (*follow, draw, and English*): AT LEAST HALF OF

YOUR SHOTS SHOULD BE CONTROLLED ONLY BY DIRECTION AND SPEED, STRIKING THE CUE BALL DEAD CENTER (and most of the time not too forcefully). However, because the spin factor seems so important, this elegant principle is often forgotten.

Now all you need are (fascinating) years of practice. And let's be realistic. There are plateaus and other intriguing facts beyond these (jump shots, throw shots, massé shots, etc.), but you have to start the climb somewhere.

◆ How to Take Your Own Pulse ◆

Any book that purports to cover a wide range of life activities can only be enhanced by a chapter about something happening inside our bodies.

I have discovered that many people do not know how to take their own pulse. It's easier to do than brushing one's teeth, and much easier than trimming one's fingernails. That you can get important information about your physical system by a very simple procedure that takes about fifteen *seconds* to learn should be of some interest. It's *your* pulse, and "your" has a more penetrating meaning in this case than, for instance, "your" sneakers or "your" computer.

How to Do It

In this exercise/cholesterol/heart-condition-aware world, we should all know how to "take our pulses," which means to determine the number of pulse beats—i.e., heartbeats—per minute. The way most recommended:

1. Place your index and middle fingers on the thumb side of your wrist, a little below the base of the thumb.

2. Press *gently* until you feel the pulse beat (if you press too hard, you may retard the beat).

3. Looking at a watch, count the number of beats during exactly fifteen seconds, and multiply this number by four. This equals the number of beats per minute—i.e., your pulse rate.

◄ **4. Don't use your thumb to feel the pulse, because it has its own pulse.** ►

Now I'm not going to produce various tables of pulse rates measured against age, activities, and so on. Why? Because I would like to encourage you to take your pulse just for the heck of it, while waiting for the bus or for the movie to begin. Check it out. It's all yours.

Optional

According to Chinese medicine, there is not one pulse, but many. The idea is that within the pulse that anybody can take after less than a minute's education, there are more subtle fluctuations going on. More specifically, in Chinese medicine it is said that there are twelve pulses, six for each wrist (taken on the radial artery), with three levels for each pulse. In addition, there are up to twenty-eight possible qualities associated with each pulse—for example, fast or slow, strong or weak, shallow or deep. Of course, it takes years to detect and interpret these.

Without taking sides, I don't consider this unreasonable. For example, there are amazingly subtle inflections in our voices that one can learn to hear more and more acutely—not to mention "overtones" that musicians recognize and that many nonmusicians do not, until they "learn" to hear them. Wonderfully intricate flavors "deep" in wine are savored more and more precisely through practice.

I know that there are many Western medical practitioners who go beyond normal skepticism and consider all of this pulse business silly. But there are also many Western medical practitioners who pay regular visits to their Chinese-medical counterparts.

◆ Guide to Some Common Tricky ◆ Points of Punctuation

A human being is an animal that punctuates.

If you are expecting a complete guide to punctuation, this isn't it. Everyone knows that there are numerous excellent books on grammar, punctuation, and style. They feature great authorities, vampires (really), and other lesser authorities. A few of my modest pages couldn't begin to compete with these dashing volumes. This chapter merely references a few of the *trickier points* that constantly cause confusion.

Use a Comma

If a string of adjectives modifies the same noun, and if "and" could be used between them without chang-

ing the meaning. A careful, wealthy daredevil; a slick, stupid astronomer. **But:** a popular lion tamer.

In dates. May 2, 1503. **BUT:** 2 May 1503 or May 1503.

To avoid obvious confusion. After you left, Pegasus bounded out of the window without cleaning up his mess. (As opposed to implying you ended a relationship with Pegasus.)

***Do not* use a comma (or a period) after a question mark or exclamation point**—even if the sentence would normally require one. He asked himself, "Am I an authority?" though he knew he wasn't a vampire.

—— *What About the Serial Comma?* ——

Bacchus bought books, bagels, and beer. Why is there sometimes a comma after "bagels" and sometimes not?

This comma is called "the serial comma," and most authorities agree that using it or not using it are both acceptable—even though ignoring it is sometimes confusing (and actually irrational). Whatever my opinion is, the way it actually breaks down in practice is that **in books the serial comma is generally used,** and **in newspapers and magazines it is not.** In your private life, you may do what you like (so far).

—————— *Use an Apostrophe* ——————

For plurals of letters or abbreviations—where not adding one would be confusing: p's and q's; M.B.A.'s.

To show possession for a proper name ending with "s." Gus's frog, the Jones's scorpion.

No extra "s" with ancient Greek names of more than one syllable that already end in "s"—Perseus' elephant, Archimedes' boa.

Italics and Double Quotes—
When to Use Which?

QUOTES
For a title of a book series: "The Hardy Boys."

ITALICS
For an actual book title: *The Disappearing Floor.*

QUOTES
For chapters or other divisions: "Chet Walks on Air."

ITALICS (GENERAL LIST FOR REFERENCE)
Book titles, plays, epic poems, major musical compositions and artistic works, magazines, newspapers, movies, radio and television shows (not individual); plaintiff and defendant in legal cases; genus and species in biological names; names of ships and aircraft, but *not space vehicles* (?!).

EXAMPLES
Lenore and the Raven, a new musical; Picasso's *Guernica*; *Monday-Night Football*; *Dick vs. Jane*; *Jabberwockus manxomus*; *Air Force One*, but Voyager II.

QUOTES (GENERAL LIST)
Titles of articles, short stories, poems, songs and short musical pieces, individual radio and TV shows.

"A Study of 19th-Century Raven Riddles"; "Lenore and the Raven," a recently discovered poem by W. S. Gilbert; "Eleanor Rigby"; "Phantom of the Sports Arena," tonight on Channel 2.

ITALICS

When you are *emphasizing* a word. (Except in this book, use sparingly.)

QUOTES

When a word or its meaning is itself the subject under discussion—or when a word is employed in a special way.

EXAMPLES

"Synthesis" is actually a *synthesis* of two words. Some poems allow you to "drink" in their words.

ITALICS

For referring to individual numbers, letters, and even words, especially if a text contains numerous instances.

If italics are not available—as in a handwritten letter or on some word processors or printers—you can use underlines, though quotes may be less fussy and more attractive. There is room for personal decision here.

Put commas and periods INSIDE quotation marks? In the United States, yes: He loved the new television show "Blank Screen." (In the United Kingdom, they do not encourage this totally bizarre practice.)

Put semicolons and colons OUTSIDE quotation marks. Other punctuation, such as exclamation points and question marks, should be put inside only if belonging to the quote (which makes sense).

174

Names of planets, stars, constellations, and galaxies.

Names of geographic regions and special structures. The South, the Continental Divide, the Western Hemisphere, the Brooklyn Bridge, the Borscht Belt.

Days, months, holidays, and special days.

Organizations, historical events, and awards. The Senate, the Boston Tea Party, the Order of the Garter.

Family relationships when used as part of the name. Aunt Boris.

BUT: My aunt, Boris.

References to the President and Vice President of the United States.

The genus part of genus/species names, and all categories higher than genus (i.e., family, order, class, phylum): genus/species—*Jabberwockus manxomus*; family—Hideosus; order—Monstera; etc.

***Do not capitalize* compass points**—unless you are referring to a definite region. "Young man, I told you to go west off the exit."

BUT: "Seek the West, young man."

***Do not capitalize* proper names that have passed into common parlance with new meanings:** dutch treat.

BUT: Dutch oven, London broil.

***Do not capitalize* the first word of the second part of a "split" direct quotation** (if it doesn't begin a sentence): "They actually asked me if I knew," said the lyricist, "if my true love was true."

◆ How to Read Faster (and Better) ◆

"Sleep faster, we need the pillows."
Yiddish proverb

We are dealing here with material that can be read relatively quickly—not poetry or technical material that must be savored and pondered as you go.

The Two Major Problems

Retracing words and phrases. Instead of continuing on when reading a line, the reader is unable to stop rereading words already read.

Making too many eye movements per line. Instead of three or four eye movements, the reader makes five or six (or even more).

Behind these well-known stumbling blocks lies the Fear of One's Unknown Capabilities. But instead of presenting you immediately with the AMAZING SOLUTION (below), you will progress even faster if you understand that what holds you back is that you don't know about . . .

> **The Law of Circuses:** To learn a new physical skill is to transform the utterly impossible into the unfailingly real.

For example, every circus has performers who *routinely* do the seemingly impossible. At some stage, even for these virtuosos, it was impossible that they could jump up from a

176

tightrope, somersault numerous times in thin air, and land back on the rope on two feet with a flourish. If you or I watch something like this unfold, it defies every bodily experience we've ever had. Though it may be called "magic," the *Law of Circuses* just considers it "learning."

Preparation for the Amazing Solution

Consider reading as a fundamentally physical activity just like walking, typing, or riding a bicycle. All of these were once "impossible." As you try to read in a new way, the idea is to recognize—in fact, to be convinced—that you have encountered this feeling of impossibility many times before, and in each case, after everything became real (and easy) the feeling of the impossible evaporated like yesterday's dew.

Welcome the "impossible," your honest adversary who, by The Law of Circuses, must give way when you start to engage.

The Moving Finger Reads— The Amazing Solution

USE YOUR FINGER TO PACE YOUR VISION ACROSS EACH LINE Place your finger right under the type and move it continually forward. With your eyes, you follow the line of type at the speed your finger is moving. The idea is to move the finger *just a little faster than you think you can read.* You will experience:

1a. A desire to retrace your words, and/or

1b. an urge to use more eye movements per line— but you don't need to.

2. The anxiety that you won't remember anything —but you will. * And most of all:

3. The utter fear that you can comprehend a passage, reading faster, without knowing how you did it! This is the real problem; the rest is just mechanics.

Reading is more "physical" than you might think. You have to exercise as if you're playing a game or a sport. To do the "impossible," you have to do it first and analyze it afterward. In the beginning, don't give a thought to how you can do this impossible thing, just keep at it and take courage from the fact that millions—billions—of people before you have gone through this and have successfully learned. The Law of Circuses applies. The impossible becomes the real every day all over the Earth.

You do have to practice. Take a definite amount of time every day to do this, starting with at least fifteen minutes. Begin with simple material: magazines, newspapers, easy novels.

At first you may not understand a lot of what you read, but after practicing this way for a week—extending the time a little every few days—you will begin to comprehend *even better than before*.

Meaning is not in the words on the paper (or in waveforms of speech for that matter). Words invoke meanings, mysteriously. That's why you can flow across the line of words and get what's there *because you aren't in charge of invoking the meaning*. You're just learning to engage your visual faculty to allow the "invoking mechanism" to operate faster (or something like that).

Reading can change your life to an important degree. (It could also be the best preparation for joining a circus.)

---

* And so what? It's just an experiment. Remember, it's only an experiment, okay?

After a while you can experiment with "speed reading." To do this, simply move your finger down the page in a zigzag fashion (or any way that works for you), taking in large gulps of material. You will be surprised at how rapidly you begin to comprehend. But practice on simple material first.

For best results, do this only as a lark.

What to Do If You're on
♦ Someone's Sailboat and You ♦
Know Nothing and You're a Klutz

There are two kinds of sailboats: **Type 1.** Boats that are thirty-five feet long or longer. On these boats, you can get chilly. **Type 2.** Boats that are under thirty-five feet. On these boats, you can get wet (and chilly). But if you wear the proper clothing, the elements aren't a problem.

How to Do It

1. Clothing. The key is to wear layers, at least three or four. On Type 1 boats, the outer garment should shield you from the wind. An ordinary "windbreaker" may not do the job. A good slicker, or a pretty heavy coat, will. On Type 2 boats, don't wear anything that can't get wet. (This doesn't mean you will probably get wet, but you could.)

2. Life preservers. It is, of course, doubtful that you will ever need one, but you must *know where they are*. If you are especially jumpy, or if you just like communications work, you might ask to have the radio explained (if there is one).

Sailing Away

3. The helmsman (or helmsperson) of yore. The helmsman, who is often the actual captain and we shall consider him or her as such, is the CEO of the boat, which includes being in charge of seating arrangements and any marriages that are performed.

IF THE CAPTAIN ASKS YOU TO CHANGE SIDES (FOR WEIGHT-BEARING REASONS—OR POSSIBLY FOR MARRIAGE REASONS), PLEASE DO THIS AT ONCE.

4. The boom. This is the large piece of wood parallel to the water to which the bottom of the mainsail is attached. **When sitting near the boom,** *keep down*—under the **path of its swing.**

5. The wind. The fundamental "given" in sailing is the direction of the wind, and you will quickly observe that when the captain turns the sailboat's front (bow) or rear (stern) from one side of the wind to the other, the sail and therefore the boom shifts around, often rapidly.

An important captain's call is "Coming about!" (the bow is going across the wind). *Coming about* is the most common way of turning across the wind.

Another important call is "Jibe!" (the stern is going across the wind). *Jibing* is less common and you should be even more alert if you hear this. ◄ *Be sure you are absolutely below the boom and out of the captain's way.* ► When a boat jibes, the boom can whip around extremely fast.

6. "Running" lines, halyards, sheets. These terms all refer to various kinds of ropes on a boat. If you come across a moving rope (it may look like a snake), ◄ *do not touch it.* ► I assure you that it's moving for an important reason. (Also, it can burn your fingers.)

7. One hand on the boat—one hand for yourself. This means that when you're moving about the boat, try to keep one hand in contact with the boat. Should there be a sudden lurch, it will be easier to get a firmer hold.

8. Seasickness. If you think you may get seasick, or if you feel a bout of nausea coming on, *do not go below* (if there is a "below"). Stay topside. Why? Because one of the contributing factors to this unpleasant condition is disorientation. If you can see something that anchors your view, you have a better chance to make it through. If you think you *might* even get seasick, once out on the waves, *do not go below at all.* I must add that if a passenger becomes seasick, it casts a pall over the entire outing. If you are so prone, there are two interesting devices to look into. One is an unobtrusive anti-nausea patch placed on the neck *an hour before departure*, which has prevented many people from experiencing this misery. There are also special bracelets. These may be found in marine supply stores.

9. The head. I'm sorry to have to introduce this unpleasant subject, but it is so important that it can't be left out. The head (toilet) on many sailboats has a lever, or valve, that the user must first push *all the way in one direction* to let water into the bowl. After the deposit is made, the valve is pushed *all the way to the other side* to flush. It is crucial that the valve not get stuck in the middle. Should this happen—or if you find it in that state when you arrive—do not attempt to force or fix anything, regardless of your phenome-

181

nal handiness ashore. If you try, a *truly horrible* situation (I'm sure you understand what I mean) can and probably will arise. Immediately go topside and report the problem to the captain, no matter what he or she is occupied with. Believe me, that person will thank you for your good sense—if not right then, soon afterward.

10. Docking. During the docking process, your desire to excel with brave deeds may cause you to leap onto the dock or perform some other ill-timed or generally misguided task. *Don't.* The captain docks the boat *and is totally in charge.* If and when the captain tells you to do something, that's when you do it.

11. Heeling. When a sailboat is breezing along nicely, it should be heeling at an angle to the water, but not at a ridiculous angle. A sailboat is designed to sail most efficiently along its "lines," which dictates the angle (the captain has a feel for this). But if the boat is heeling so far over that water is almost creeping or is creeping over the side, then the captain should know that this is actually inefficient sailing, and it's time to change to a smaller sail or "reef" (i.e., to shorten up) the present sail. But I don't believe the captain will appreciate your sage advice. You might, however, cleverly engage this daredevil in a discussion of "sailboat heeling." Maybe he'll get the idea (if you're not the least pushy about it).

Generally, heeling is an important and charming contributor to the joy of sailing.

12. Bad captains and pleasant sailing don't mix. One of the captain's responsibilities is to put his or her passengers at ease, even when forceful commands have to be given. If a captain is overdomineering, abusive, or reckless, you will find a way to decline the next invitation. Being a guest on such a boat is neither pleasant nor intelligent.

◆ How to Save Receipts ◆

Some of you will be puzzled that a grown person could have the least difficulty putting little pieces of paper with numbers and other crypto-accounting phenomena in a safe place for future retrieval. You are the happy ones, the ones who breeze through.

How could you possibly understand our bizarre problem? How can you explain that, for instance, some of us can go out and supervise—with 360° vision and total efficiency—a hundred men and women who might be constructing a nuclear reactor or a movie set, and yet fumble in search of a crumpled restaurant receipt?

Perhaps you've tried all the fancy items in office supply stores that are supposed to help you save receipts. The problem is that these were designed by people *who already save receipts*. Yet there is one item you may have overlooked, which was created by someone *who knows about us:*

1. Obtain an open manilla envelope with a stiff wide bottom so you can STUFF it full of receipts. That's it. That's the secret.

2. Place it in "partitioners" on top of your desk— or in some other accessible location.

3. When the envelope gets filled up, pour the contents into a regular *clasp* envelope. Scribble the current year on both its sides, and . . .

4. Return the now empty original envelope to its place to await more fodder.

You laugh, you who already know. Well, armed with our envelopes, we shall rise up, break the chains, and salvage receipts that you never knew existed.

Optional

Splurge. Buy one or two more of these miracle envelopes (in different colors). Put them in the partitions. Then think of other paper pieces to stuff into these happy containers. For example, if you are a checkbook balancer, your *automatic teller receipts.*

You're on your own.

How to Instantly Figure an Annual ◆ Salary from an Hourly Wage

Something you always wanted to know, but you didn't know you could know.

How to Do It

To figure an annual salary, double the hourly wage and add three zeroes.

EXAMPLE:	$12/hour	Double it,
	24	and add three zeroes (or "K").
RESULT:	$24,000 or 24K.	

To figure the hourly wage, do the opposite.

EXAMPLE:	$44,650	Simplify,
	44	and take half.
RESULT:	$22/hour	

Extremely Optional

This method works because there are 2,000 annual hours, based on an 8-hour day, a 40-hour week, and a "50"-week year. To multiply a number by 2,000, double it and add three zeroes.

◆ Directions for Screwing ◆

What is the BIG SECRET of screwing?

Also, how can you remember which direction screws screw in, and more important, when they're tightly engaged, in which direction do they screw *out?**

How to Do It

The Big Secret. JUST BEFORE YOU SCREW SCREWS INTO WOOD, RUB AN OLD PIECE OF *SOAP* OVER THE THREADS. Yep, that's it. Every woodworking human employs this trick and it ACTUALLY ALWAYS WORKS. You can't believe how easy it makes screwing. Ordinary old soap—any bar. Every carpenter worth his salt keeps a bar in his toolbox. (For fine work, some carpenters use beeswax since soap may slightly discolor a natural finish.)

Two Kinds of Common Screwdrivers. In case you weren't sure, there are regular screwdrivers and Phillips screwdrivers (named after Mr. and Mrs. Phillips). (See "Basic Tools," pg. 201, if you need brief descriptions.)

Screwing Directions. To make matters clearer, when removing a screw we will not say "screw out," but instead we will say "screw OFF" (an easily remembered phrase). And therefore when tightening a screw, we will not say "screw in," but "screw ON."

---

* You who deal with concepts like screws or screwdrivers should not be smug. Many people who rarely do can nevertheless do things you would cringe at.

Why? Because almost everyone opens and closes lids every day. And lids are screwed OFF and ON the same way screws are screwed OFF and ON (counterclockwise and clockwise, respectively).

The Mighty Dime

Hundreds of years from now, hopefully thousands (but nothing lasts forever), when North America is finally a large theme park, those who really know what's important will look back and recognize that the United States was the country that brought a new concept of liberty, a new dessert (strawberry shortcake, invented by Yankee pioneers), jazz, and the *dime*—the most useful object any government ever made available to its citizens. The dime, being the screwdriver of choice for many small jobs, especially when you don't have a screwdriver in the vicinity, will continue in the future to rescue both lives and weddings as a result of its use in emergency repairs.

Perhaps the Mercury dime will come back, one of the most beautiful pieces of twentieth-century money the United States ever minted.

◆ How to Tie Your Shoes ◆

"So he stood in his shoes
And he wonder'd.
He wonder'd,
He stood in his shoes
And he wonder'd."
John Keats, from "A Song About Myself"

When your shoes come untied, you always think it's the shoelaces (sometimes it is). And you think that the only way to protect yourself in critical situations is to tie a "double knot," i.e., to tie the two bows together with an extra over-hand knot, which looks bulky. Well, they never told you that all your life you've been tying *the wrong knot.* Don't feel neglected. What you also didn't know was that according to an (independent) survey, *one-fourth of all North Americans tested tie their shoes wrong.*

The situation is easy to diagnose. If shoes are well tied, the laces lie *straight across* the shoe in a Square Knot.* If poorly tied, the laces usually form the dreaded Granny Knot and lie *diagonally across* the shoe, or *up and down.*

Unfortunately, the Granny Knot comes undone at fiend-ishly important occasions, i.e., occasions when items tend to come undone or be missing.†

* Though this chapter is self-contained, for a description of the Square Knot and Granny Knot, see "Knots You Need, and Knots You Don't," pg. 111.
† Examples of Fiendishly Important Occasions are your day before a Congressional committee, the business deal of your life, your first date with the girl or boy of your dreams, your coronation.

EMBARRASSMENT QUOTIENTS FOR FIENDISHLY IMPORTANT OCCASIONS (EXCERPT)

Fly Open	89
Shoelace Untied	*89*
Hair in Curlers	82
Shirttail Out	72
Missing Belt on Suit (no suspenders)	55
Missing Cuff Button	55
Necktie (with food spot)	54
Necktie (with two food spots)	53 (may pass as part of a pattern)
Ugly Hat	50
One Shoe Missing	23 (commonly considered a sign of gutsy eccentricity—or an injured foot)

Test Yourself

Tie your shoes your usual way. *Check the laces.* If they lie straight across your shoe, you are free to go. But if they lie diagonally across, or up and down, you need to know . . .

How to Tie Your Shoes (So They Won't Come Undone)

We all begin tying a shoe with an Overhand Knot. *But there are two kinds of Overhand Knots:* one that starts with the right-hand lace in front of the left, i.e., right-over-left, or the one that starts the opposite way, with left-over-right.

Whichever kind of Overhand Knot you begin with—if

you've been tying your shoes wrong all your life—*then reverse the way you tie the first overhand knot*. Then proceed the way you always do. *That's it, no more shoelace agony.*

Sure, occasionally there really are dumb shoelaces that come undone no matter which one of these knots you tie, but in that case, GET NEW SHOELACES. Until you do, tie the proper knot, then using the two "bows" as ends, tie an *additional* Overhand Knot (of either type). This is the usual way that many people know, and it's not totally foolproof. But there is another way known almost exclusively by explorers and zealous hikers . . .

The Amazing Secret Method of Tying Your Shoes—with Genuinely Lousy Shoelaces (So They Won't Come Undone)

After you make the beginning overhand knot, form a loop or "bow" with one lace, and wrap the other lace once around that bow, then *wrap it once more around the bow*. Finish the regular way.

How to Tie Your Shoes from Scratch

If I were to describe in detailed words the most common, correct method used to tie shoelaces, its sheer complexity would put you to sleep at once.

How complicated, really, is tying your shoes? You can test this right now. Look at what you're doing when you tie your shoes. It's like an intricate dance step. For example, observe

190

the way your fingers are *pulling* loops, *making* loops, and *adjusting* their lengths—all at the same time. Did you *really* know you could do this? Notice how the two hands have to coordinate their actions to arrive at the end of the pulling movement at the same moment—otherwise, a loops falls apart. Very elegant. There is probably a mathematical theorem waiting to be discovered here about noninterfering, co-operative movements.)

However, given the subtitle of this book, my publisher would, understandably, never permit me to get away without some legitimate, complete description of shoe tying. So here is a very easy method to read and to understand. But it's boring compared to the one most of us actually use.

1. Start with both laces roughly the same length.

2. Tie an Overhand Knot of either type—i.e., one-half a Square or Granny Knot.

3. Form a loop or *bow* at the end of each lace.

4. Hold a loop in each hand, as if each were a single strand, and tie a second Overhand Knot *of the opposite type*. (This makes a Square Knot).

5. Tighten by pulling on the loops.

Of course, all you've done is tie a Square Knot—with bows! No matter how you tie your shoes, a Square Knot is the key.

The Law of Shoelaces: If you need string in an emergency— or to show a child how to tie a knot—use your shoelace.*

* Okay, so it's more of a suggestion than a law.

The Wonderful World of Tidal Creatures

This is the truth! In variety, bizarreness (to us, not to them), exotic beauty, and *names*, tidal creatures are the equal of any grouping of anything living or dead on Earth.

I admit that I'm crazy about these beings, and in my fanaticism I have obscured any sort of scientific approach. But I mean no harm.

Where Are They?

Tidal creatures are all around the edges of water doing their very important work, while being utterly fascinating to anyone who cares to look or otherwise get involved. They're found on beaches with outcroppings of rock that create tide-pools—when the tide recedes—such as on our northern coasts. Turn over various sized rocks (Always put them back, and *carefully!* Otherwise, you not only destroy homes and ultimately creatures, but also put so much stress on the microecosystem that it will take *years* for it to come back to life.) Tidal creatures are found in shallow waters of some sandy coasts, as well as in beds of seaweed and around pilings. Tidal creatures are even in good aquarium stores (go at once).

Here are a few examples out of *millions*:

The Ice Cream Cone Worm. Sound stupid? Wrong! This sagacious animal actually *selects* extremely even-sized grains of sand and stores them (somewhere) until it gets enough to add another ring to its perpetually growing ice-cream-cone-shaped tube that it makes out of a single layer of very fine sand grains. It connects them together with this glue (okay, so it's mucus). A tad more than 1½″ long, it is creamy pink speckled with red and blue. The tubes stick up in the sand.

How about a **Boring Sponge**? No kidding, that's its name. It consists of huge numbers of little sponges ⅛″ wide that cluster together (when you're bored you seek company). I definitely don't want to say anything negative because these creatures secrete *sulfuric acid*—but fortunately (for us) only onto shells and coral. The acid breaks up the host into tiny particles, and all of this helps make sandy beaches so other creatures can live pleasantly—or unpleasantly—and you and I can go swimming.

No one should forget to invite a **Giant Feather Duster** to a party. These are art-institute worms that live in durable parchmentlike tubes. When you get a lot of them conferencing, you get a giant reddish-hued feather duster! But they can retract into their tubes almost as fast as a computer system can go down—for instance, when a *shadow* passes over them.

For special situations, both **Slime** and **Large-Eyed Feather Dusters** are available. And for exalted occasions, you can get a **Magnificent Feather Duster** (that's really the name).

193

The Trumpet Stalked Jellyfish has a brightly colored, trumpet-shaped body. It attaches itself with its center stalk to objects underwater by means of an adhesive pad at the tip. (The first Post-It?) This creature is only 1″ high, but still manages to possess *four lips*. Thus, it not only has a trumpet shape, but probably could be a great trumpet *player* if given half a chance.

Bushy-Backed Sea Slugs, Northern Basket Stars, Ghost Anemones, Zigzag Wine-Glass Hydroids, Bushy Wine-Glass Hydroi— Hold it right there! You're making these up, that's what.

I am not. And if you think *these* are unusual, how about some of their *real* (scientific) names—like *California sticho-pus?* A Tidal Convention is quite an event:

Hello, I'm *Crossaster papposus* (for some reason, their last names always start with a small letter) and you?

I'm *Cleona celata!* And you thought I was *boring!*

Makes the names of rock groups seem tame.*

---

* Rockers—another multimillion-dollar idea—gratis.

194

◆ How to Figure a 15 Percent Tip ◆

--------- *A Typical Problem—* ---------
Restaurant Chagrin

You're in one of those restaurants where you're afraid that
the waiter is more sophisticated than you are. It's your
check, and you suddenly have to figure the tip. Since your
reputation as a restaurant maven is on the line, you want to
do this unobtrusively. Here is the classic method. After a
few goof-ups you'll have it down perfectly.

The key word is *approximately*. To figure a 15% tip:

What to Do	*How to Do It*
1. Divide the total by 10.	Remove the last digit and forget the decimal point: $31.67 = *316*
2. Divide the answer to Step 1 by 2.	You only have to do this *approximately*: 316/2 = *158* (or "*150*")
3. The answer to Step 1 + the answer to Step 2 is the answer.	Do this *approximately*. Put decimal point in obvious place and round to nearest $.25: 310 + 150 = 460. Hence, *475* or *$4.75*.*

* You know it's not $475. And $47.50 is still more than the original bill. But $4.75 seems
right. In today's world, $.47, let alone, $.04, isn't going to make it.

Step 1 is 10 percent.
Step 2 is 5 percent (by a mathematical trick!).
Step 3 makes 15 percent.

How to Change a Tire

Unscrew something, replace it with something else, screw it back on. Millions upon millions of people have changed tires without mishap and so can you.

Basic Difficulties

I will get horribly dirty. (Roll up your sleeves. Put something down for your knee to rest on.)

I will be humiliated by passing motorists who will see that I am gauche. (By and large, no one cares because they're all going somewhere important.)

I will be sucked into oncoming traffic by the wind of passing cars. (Anyone who has changed a tire on a freeway knows that this is a good point. Therefore, if you weigh less than two pounds, do not attempt to change your tire.)

The car will fall on me and I will die. (You're absolutely wrong. You have no business getting under the car when it's jacked up for any reason whatsoever even if your favorite object has rolled underneath.)

How to Do It

1. **Drive to level ground.** For automatic transmissions, put car in park; for manual transmissions, put in reverse or first gear.

2. **Set the emergency brake.** For complete safety, put a block (a brick or rock) under the wheel opposite.

3. **Get the jack, jack base, lug wrench, and spare tire out of the truck.** *Everything feels cold and clammy.*

4. **Pry the hubcap off with flat end of your lug wrench, just as you would a paint can or jam jar.**

◄ 5. *Loosen lug nuts with a wrench.* ► (This is the core of the whole procedure, elaborated in its own section below.)

6. **Stand bumper jack straight up and down in its base.** Some jacks are inserted into a special notch or recess in the frame. These are even easier to work. Get the owner's

manual out and check which kind you have. Otherwise, about a foot from the end of the bumper nearest the flat:

7. Engage the jack in some reasonable fashion under the bumper. (You may think this is a sticky point. It isn't, since almost any reasonable engagement will do.)

8. Flip lever up and insert flat end of your lug wrench in socket of jack, and pump the lever up and down.

9. If jack tilts from vertical in either direction, *lower car*, *readjust jack*, and start over.

10. When tire is an inch or so from ground, remove the *already loosened lug nuts*. ◀ Put them in the hubcap so they won't get away. ▶

11. Remove the flat tire and put on the spare. If you observe how you take off the flat, then you'll easily know how to put the spare on. Another example of The Great Law of Undoing (pg. 121).

12. Put nuts back and screw finger-tight only, alternating according to the illustration.

13. Lower car by flipping lever down and then pumping it again with your lug wrench.

14. When tire hits the ground, finish tightening nuts. Do not grind them to mush. Either bang the hubcap back onto the wheel (with your hand or foot), or put it on the front seat as a reminder to get the flat fixed.

How to Loosen the Lug Nuts

Insert the socket of the lug wrench on one of the nuts, apply force counterclockwise* (grunting if necessary), or step on the wrench and apply body weight. *Or jump on the wrench.* In desperation, find a longer piece of metal and use it as a hammer or a lever. (If you don't know what a lever is, you'll find out very quickly and never forget.)

Optional

Now continue on to the wedding with a deservedly inflated ego. Especially if it's raining, which it often is.

---

* A few cars' lug nuts screw the *other* way. Very few, though. (Check your manual if you are having difficulty.)

How to Plunge a Toilet (to Unclog It)

Let's not waste time on niceties.

How to Do It

Any plunger is welcome at a time like this, but for toilets get one that has an extra "fold" in the middle.

1. Hold the plunger like you would a broom, only a little more firmly.

2. Position the rubber suction cup directly over the flush-hole in the bottom of the toilet bowl.

3. *Plunge*—i.e., push up and down on the handle for fifteen or twenty seconds.

4. Pull the plunger up off the hole sharply to "pull" up any obstruction. The suction keeps the cup sucked down in position while plunging, and it also sucks up whatever might be clogged, allowing it to break up in a natural way.

If nothing happens, continue plunging in twenty- or thirty-second stretches.

Optional

After a few more minutes, if the toilet is still clogged, you have two choices:

You can continue on with an auger (a wire thing), a

snake,* or a home-made wire thing, or . . .

You can call a plumber (or a friend who has an auger, a snake, or a home-made wire thing).

Yet I have always found that simple plunging goes a long way. So this chapter stops here.

Basic Tools

"Every tool carries with it the spirit by which it was created."
Werner Heisenberg from *Physics and Philosophy*

* This is not a live snake, but a slithery wire cable that insinuates itself downward into obtuse crevices where "clog" is lurking.

Without taking into account any special needs (your home is made of wool, or you plan to construct antique mahogany cabinets), here is a reasonable—and graded—list of the basic, all-purpose tools and accessories.

I assume that you have such items as scissors, transparent tape, string, a stapler, and WD-40 (or other household oil). The following also doesn't include painting supplies, finishes, or gardening tools.

– *Very Short List (All-Purpose Tools)* –

MATT KNIFE OR EQUIVALENT CUTTING OBJECT
A knife in whatever form is the world's most used implement.

Emergency alternate: nail clippers, single-edge razor blade, kitchen knife.

SCREWDRIVER
This is probably the second most-used tool around the house, and there are two kinds: a regular screwdriver for normal-looking screws, and a Phillips screwdriver for double-slotted screws (you can use a small regular for Phillips screws, but it's not as effective).

One regular screwdriver is enough for a very basic collection, but it's a better idea to have a set of various sizes—at least two or three—and at least one Phillips if you are going to do any decent amount of screwing. If the tip is too small for the screw—and it's a difficult screw—you can easily mush up the slot, making it *really* hard to get off. *Include an old piece of soap* to make screws go in easier. (See "Directions for Screwing," pg. 186.)

Emergency alternate: a dime.

HAMMER AND/OR TACK HAMMER (MAGNETIC!)

Every home needs something modest that can hit things. A *magnetic tack hammer* is perfect. (Some people actually use this hammer more often than a "real" one.) With this nifty tool, you can nail little nails and brads and tacks that are too small to hold in position. The head is magnetic, so you place the end of the tack on the head of the hammer and *it sticks there*. Then you tap it into where it's going without having it drop behind the piano.

Emergency alternate: shoe (for tacks and brads only), old iron skillet, heavy metal.

PLIERS/ADJUSTABLE WRENCH

For tightening nuts and especially for removing nuts from bolts—and screwing off and screwing on larger objects, like shower heads. Use for pulling out difficult nails or for anything you need to grip, twist, or pull. You may also need pliers or a wrench in your home for turning off the main gas shutoff. Use a rag on items you don't want scratched or marred.

Emergency alternate: hands (holding a towel), heavy-duty can opener with rubber-coated handles—used upside-down (coating provides an excellent grip).

ADHESIVES, GLUE

White glue and/or any of the mass-market super adhesives. *Packing Tape* —there's wide brown "post office" tape and extremely strong transparent fibery-looking "strapping tape." *Electrical Tape* for modest emergencies if you have to insulate (cover up) visibly damaged wires. Don't use electrical tape inside the walls. (I can't picture you in there yet, but who knows?)

**WHATEVER OTHER TAPE YOU LIKE
TO USE—PERHAPS DUCT TAPE**

This is a silver-gray tape that sticks to almost *anything*. The more you use it, the more indispensable it is.

MEASURING TAPE

There will always come a time when you need one. Get one in a metal casing, at least 8 feet long. ◄ In tight spots, *use the metal casing as part of the rule*, which is usually 2″ wide. ► (NOTE: In heftier models, it may be 2½″ or even 3″.)

Emergency alternates: Standard typing paper is 8½″ by 11″ (note that this is one inch less than a foot). Can be folded in half. *Dollar bills* (and up) are exactly 6⅛″ × 2½″.

Learn to "walk off" a yard by checking your personal tread. Also, know the width of *your own stretched hand*, from thumb-tip to the tip of your little finger. This is particularly useful because it's so handy to apply.

A SHOCKING SUGGESTION

It's much easier than you think to *memorize* short lengths. "Learn" how long a foot is without referring to a ruler. (Would you believe, you already know?) Then it's a child's game to "cut it in half" to get 6″. And everyone should "know" the length of an inch. The funny thing is that all you need to do is to *decide* to learn how to do this. How about right now?

―――― *Almost on the Short List* ――――

ELECTRIC DRILL (MOTOR) AND DRILL BITS

This may be the easiest power tool to use. If the thought of power tools bothers you, start with this one. A real time-saver. Great for putting up shelves and lots of other items. If you buy one with variable speeds, it can double as an automatic screwdriver.

ASSORTED NAILS AND SCREWS
These appear from nowhere like paper clips.

SANDPAPER
You should have fine, medium, and coarse. Always double-fold sandpaper when you use it. Or better, get a *Sanding Block*.

WIRE CUTTER/STRIPPER
There is a combination tool that does both (you can also use a knife). If you have to do any fooling around with wires (speakers, lamps, etc.), then you should definitely have one of these.

Continuing the List
——— *(It Never Really Ends)* ———

PUTTY KNIFE
Use with *spackle*, for example, to repair cracks and holes in walls before painting.

AWL
Use with hammer to start small screw-holes and for poking holes; e.g., in belts, and for general poking around.

PENCILS
For marking, keep in a handy place—for example . . .

A TOOL CHEST

The Law of Hardware Stores: Most humans cannot resist purchasing something when visiting a hardware (or stationery) store.

◆ How to Tuck Your Shirt In ◆

There are two general ways to tuck your shirt in. One of them doesn't work (the shirt tends to come out); the other one works (the shirt tends to stay in).

How to Do It

WHAT DOESN'T WORK
Shove the shirt down between your belt-line and your underwear.

WHAT WORKS
Reach into trousers through the fly, and on one side hold on to the bottom of the shirt as far around toward your back as possible, then *pull it down* into position. Do the same for the other side.

Amazing. It's that simple.

◆ How to Wash Windows at Home ◆

One of the best domestic two-person jobs: one on the outside, one on the inside, washing the same unit of window space at the same time. (For couples it can be a rather intimate experience.) Also, the notion of cleaning something essentially invisible is ironically appealing.

How to Do It

One of the reasons cosmic beings caused newspapers to be invented was to have something handy for people to wash windows with. Newspapers are really good, as long as you have gloves (like dishwashing gloves). Gloves? Because the newsprint comes off all over your hands, but it doesn't come off on the windows. In fact, there's something about the "granularity" of newsprint that gets windows squeaky clean. (I suppose clean **lintless** rags also work—I wouldn't know.)

The two classical cleaners are Windex (or one of the perfectly good similar products)—or ammonia and water. Unfortunately ammonia and water stinks, but it's very effective.

Of course, if you're out of everything, you can always *cheat* and use baking soda. It's cheating because of . . .

The Law of Baking Soda: Baking soda happens to work on everything, in everything, and for everything, which makes it unfair to other perfectly decent products.

APPLY CLEANER BY SPRAY OR RAG, WASHING A PORTION OR A PANE AT A TIME.

A classical difficulty in washing a windowpane is that you often get streaks while drying,* and since a windowpane is invisible, you can't tell which side the streaks are actually on. You rub it and it just sits there—especially if it's a one-person job. A how-to-do-it trick comes to the rescue:

The inside person makes *horizontal* strokes.

The outside person makes *vertical* strokes—even if you're the same person. (ELEGANT SOLUTIONS WAIT TO BE DISCOVERED IN ALL DOMAINS OF LIFE.)

NOTE: The trickiest part of washing windows is when it involves *ladder work*. ◄ Don't be funny with ladders. ► Make certain they are stable below and don't go higher than recommended. Those who find it exhilarating to work up on a ladder—and many do—have no need to show off.

* "Difficulty" is stretching it a bit—perhaps "subtle dilemma" is better.

How to Serve Wine

◆   ◆

"If penicillin can cure those who are ill,
Spanish cherry can bring the dead back to life."
Sir Alexander Fleming (the discoverer of penicillin)

The Law of Civilization: Things usually move along better if questions appear before answers.

How to Do It

What's the best corkscrew? Only a fool would fall for the Corkscrew Question. Why? Because only a fool would invite "zealot mail," which is indescribably boring. You see, every brilliant and inept inventor gets "corkscrew struck"—i.e., obsessed with designing the Great International Corkscrew and zealousness follows straightaway. So we have ones that screw, ones that wind, ones that slip along the edges, and ones that pump carbon dioxide into the cork, which are supposed to work really well EXCEPT THAT OCCASIONALLY THE BOTTLE EXPLODES (not to worry—it doesn't, uh, happen too often).*

    How cold should wine be before serving? My experience is that wines are *often overchilled*. White wines should

---

* Most zealots aren't very attentive, so we'll sneak this in down here. Any kind of corkscrew that works for you is good. If you just don't know, then get a common corkscrew with "wings" on the side that move up as you screw down. Make sure the thread is *wide* and is long enough to go *all the way into the cork*. If you are going to be opening well-aged bottles of red wine that contain sediment and possibly crumbly corks, there are devices with an auxiliary screw that work more gently.

209

be served at approximately 55°, which really isn't *that* cold. Forty-five minutes in the refrigerator is sufficient. Red wines, of course, should not be chilled, but served at "room temperature," which in the food and drink world is a code word for 68° (the actual range for red wine is about 65° to 68° —if the room is cold, then you will need to warm it up, etc.).

Since wines are often stored in a cool place, ideally they should be brought into a normal room a day or so ahead of time. (This is the principle, but if you can't foresee the occasion, then just make do. Or why not try to foresee the occasion?)

Rosé and dessert wines can be *slightly* chilled, to about 60°.

Should a wine always be allowed to "breathe" before drinking? Most people agree (and you can easily test this) that almost all red wines benefit from being opened at least a half an hour or, even better, an hour or two ahead of serving time, both to dissipate "bottle odor" and to allow air to mix with the wine—a fine red, especially. But if the wine is *well-aged* (more than ten years old), then less time is needed, maybe half an hour. One wine expert I know says that if you possess a genuine "museum piece"(!), it should be opened at the table and served almost immediately because the "nose" may vanish within a few minutes.

So what about this "nose" business—should I really swirl the wine around in the glass? Is this a fake deal? Experiencing the "nose" or "bouquet" happens to be a genuine pleasure in wine drinking, and swirling the wine around in a wineglass ◄ *that should never be more than two-thirds full* ► releases the bouquet. Would you be considered a snob if you were pleased by a whiff of apple pie steaming up in front of you? However, this isn't meant to encourage ostentatious wine-swirling. It's for you, not for show.

210

Do I need to "decant" a bottle of wine? The purpose of decanting, i.e., to carefully pour off a wine that contains sediment—especially an aged red wine—into a clean bottle or decanter is to prevent unpleasant sediments from entering the glass. (An old white wine generally needs only to be stood on end a few hours before serving.)

But look, you and I know that you aren't going to be decanting anything—unless, of course, you're really "into" wine, in which case I emphasize that for you this is a Dick-and-Jane chapter on wine. (Look, Jane! Spot is swirling his dish! And so forth.)

My advice is to stand the bottle on end in a normally heated room a day in advance. The sediment should gradually sink to the bottom, making it easier to either decant or pour carefully, whatever your *wine merchant* suggests. Yes, I suggest that you establish a more knowledgeable relationship with that person, because should you pursue this interest, you will derive other benefits from it. (Incidentally, wine decanting tends to evoke "wine squabbling" among wine enthusiasts.)

What shape glasses do I really have to have? If you own only one kind of wineglass, it should be tulip-shaped. Every kind of table wine can be poured into these. If you also have on hand smaller tulip-shaped glasses for fortified wines, that's all you will need. Of course, other shapes are nice and useful to own as well.

Do I have to store wine in a cellar? Store wine in a cool, dark place with bottles on their sides (which leaves cork moist). Do not store underneath the stairs because ◄ too much jostling isn't good for wine. ►

Pouring tip. When pouring wine into a glass, do it the way a good waiter does: Finish off the pour by rotating the bottle a little. This prevents unwanted drips on the linen. It is also subtly dashing and inexplicably satisfying to do.

The Downside of Wine

Someone has received an enormous wine book for a present, almost as big as the unabridged dictionary. It has an imposing title like *Everything That Was, That Is, and That Will Ever Be Known About Wine*. This is a wonderful book chockfull of wine lore, but when the poor bloke spills wine on the new carpet and frantically pages through the index under "Cleaning Up"—you know what? It's not there! He's been tricked again!!

THE GREAT WINE BOOK RESCUE
For white-wine stains, immediately pour seltzer or club soda onto the spot. Soak up with a clean rag and let dry. If necessary, later you can apply hot water and a mild detergent.

For red-wine stains, you can sprinkle much salt on the spot (or—you guessed it—the great supersubstance, *Baking Soda*). Let stand, then use seltzer or club soda—or even water—and soak up as before.

Now, why doesn't the wine industry provide us with a number like 800-WINE OFF?*

---

* This is not preposterous. You may not realize that perhaps the greatest 800-number of all time is 800-CRAYOLA. No matter what kind of bizarre material you or your kids mess up with crayons—even if you leave a crayon in your shirt and it goes through the *dryer*—these wise beings know how to get it off. (For the dryer, it's WD-40). One can also appreciate the founders' clairvoyance, in 1903, to have selected a *seven-letter* word for the product.

How to Organize Your Life, Your Desk, and When All Else Fails, Your Miniature Zeppelin Collection

There are thousands of books about how to organize your bathroom, your closet, your garage, your life, whatever. What happens to the people who read these books? The closets, the cupboards, the life is beautiful, really "together" as some contemporary folks say—for a week or two. Then something happens, everything falls apart, and it was another good try.

What went wrong?

--------------------- *How to Do It?* ---------------------

What went wrong is the failure to understand that there are some truths more real than putting this over here and that over there—truths like

THE THREE STUPENDOUS PROPERTIES OF PERSONAL OBJECTS
  1. Personal Objects Materialize Out of Nowhere.
Where did those papers under the coffee table come from?
  2. Personal Objects Shift Around by Themselves.
Why is the telephone in the bathtub?
  3. Personal Objects Disappear into Nowhere. This one is well-known. Not much needs to be added except to note that among the synonyms for "nowhere" are "Where the paper clips and socks go," "Where the lost umbrellas live," and "The fifth dimension."*

---

* Every important law or truth always spawns secondary spin-offs which, though interesting, are rarely as elegant, reasonable, and useful as the original. Here is one that has even squashed two of the points into one and mixed up the order. (Of course, it's not very helpful since it's about things you can't even see):
  "Like all successful scientific theories, QED [Quantum Electrodynamics] is based on concepts that are really quite simple. In fact, there are only two basic assumptions:
  1. Forces are transmitted by particles.
  2. These particles can pop into existence out of nothing, and then disappear again after the force has been transmitted."
  From *The Edges of Science* by Richard Morris (Englewood Cliffs, N.J.: Prentice Hall Press, 1990), pg. 23.